RUN YOUR HOUSEHOLD LIKE A BUSINESS

BUILDING FINANCIAL STRUCTURE, DISCIPLINE, AND STABILITY AT HOME.

ERIC LAWRENCE FRAZIER MBA

Run Your Household Like a Business
Copyright © 2026 by The Power Is Now Publishing

All rights reserved. This book or parts thereof may not be reproduced in any form, stored in any retrieval system, or transmitted in any form by any means- electronic, mechanical, photocopy, recording, or otherwise-without before written permission of the publisher. For permission requests, write the publisher at the email address below.

Paperback: 978-1-949722-24-6

Disclaimer

The information in "Run Your Household Like a Business " is for general informational and educational purposes only. The content in this book is based on his personal experiences, research, and general knowledge and should not be considered professional financial advice.

Readers are encouraged to consult with a certified financial advisor, HUD-approved housing and credit counselor, or other qualified professionals before taking any action regarding their credit or financial situation. The author and publisher are not liable for any actions taken from reading this book.

Additionally, this book contains links to third-party websites for additional resources and information. These links are provided for convenience and informational purposes only. The author and publisher do not endorse or take responsibility for the content, accuracy, or reliability of any information on these external sites. The use of any third-party websites is at the reader's own risk.

By reading this book, you acknowledge and agree that the author and publisher shall not be held liable for any loss or damage, including but not limited to direct, indirect, or consequential losses, arising from the use or reliance on the information contained within this book or any third-party links referenced herein.

DEDICATION

*This book is dedicated first and foremost to my wife, **Ruby Lee Gordon Frazier**—the love of my life and my partner for forty-four years. She has been the constant center of our home and the truest example of what stability, discipline, and commitment look like when practiced daily. Long before I advised clients or wrote frameworks, our household became my first business laboratory. Together, we tested ideas in real life—through seasons of growth, challenge, sacrifice, and perseverance. Nothing in this book is theoretical to us. It was lived.*

*It is also dedicated to our **four daughters**, who taught me that leadership is not about control, but about example. Parenting makes it impossible to hide from your own inconsistencies. Our home forced clarity—what we believed, how we prioritized, and how we managed our resources had real consequences. That experience shaped everything I teach.*

*To our **five grandchildren**, this book is part of the legacy I hope to leave you. The world you are inheriting will reward those who can think clearly, plan intentionally, and lead responsibly. My hope is that you understand early what* *many learn too late: wealth is not luck, and stability is not accidental. Both are built.*

*To my **sons-in-law**, thank you for the love you show my daughters and the leadership you bring into our family. Strong households are built through shared responsibility and aligned values, not individual effort alone.*

This book is also dedicated to the families who were never given a plan. To those who worked hard, did what they were told, and still felt unprepared to manage money, responsibility, and long-term direction. The absence of a framework—not the absence of effort—is what holds most people back.

*Finally, I dedicate this work to my publishing and production team—**Kim Collier, Daniels Mungai, and Alvin Mungai**. Thank you for your research, discipline, and unwavering support. Great work is never done alone, and I value the care you brought to helping shape this message into something clear, practical, and lasting.*

No plan was given.
So one is offered here.

PREFACE

We all begin life the same way. We come from a mother and a father. However complicated or imperfect that reality may be, it is the starting point for our existence. We are born into a family, shaped by that family, and influenced—sometimes profoundly—by what we see, hear, and experience in that environment.

Our parents teach us in two ways: by what they tell us and by what they show us. They model how to work, relate, manage conflict, handle money, and navigate responsibility. Over time, those lessons—intentional or not—become our blueprint for adulthood.

Then, at some point, we leave the nest. Ideally, we are prepared. Ideally, we step into the world equipped to build a life and, for many of us, to start families of our own. But this is where a quiet and persistent problem emerges—one that cuts across income levels, cultures, and professions.

Most of us leave home without ever being taught how to *run* our lives.

It's not uncommon to see patterns repeat across generations. In some families, nearly everyone becomes a doctor, lawyer, or accountant. In others, entrepreneurship runs through the bloodline. In still others, generations work blue-collar jobs in factories, retail, or restaurants. Some families raise artists—writers, performers, musicians, creators. And occasionally, one person steps outside the pattern entirely, carving out a different path.

But regardless of the path, something critical is almost always missing.

Very few people leave home with a clear understanding of how to manage a household. How to prioritize responsibilities. How to organize money. How to think strategically about income, expenses, risk, growth, and the future. We are told to go to school, get a job, work hard, save what we can, and retire someday. Or, if we come from entrepreneurial families, we are told to build a business, make money, and create independence. In both cases, we are rarely given the *tools*.

We are not taught how to create a plan. We are not taught what that plan should include. We are not taught how to think like leaders of our own lives, responsible not just for earning money but for directing it intentionally. We are expected to figure it out as we go—often through trial and error and unnecessary hardship.

This has been my experience. It has also been the experience of the countless individuals and families I have worked with through personal financial coaching and advisory services. Over and over again, I see capable, intelligent people struggling—not because they lack discipline or effort, but because they lack a framework.

This book exists to provide the plan that was never handed to us.

It is written for those who were never taught how to run their household with clarity and structure. It is written for those who want more than survival—for those who want stability, direction, and long-term security. It is written to provide guidance, education, motivation, and inspiration, but more importantly, to establish a truth that is difficult to escape.

It is impossible to succeed in life without a plan. No plan means no direction. No direction leads to disorder. And disorder, over time, produces failure—financially, relationally, and emotionally.

Every meaningful outcome begins with design. Every structure requires a blueprint. Every business requires a plan. Every growing thing requires intentional care, nourishment, and guidance. A household is no different.

This book invites you into that design process. It challenges you to see your household not as a collection of disconnected decisions but as a system—one that must be led, governed, and stewarded intentionally.

Welcome to the plan.

Welcome to How to Run Your Household Like a Business.

BUSINESS BOOKS

ERIC LAWRENCE FRAZIER, MBA BUSINESS BOOKS

AVAILABLE ON AMAZON

POETRY COLLECTION

ERIC LAWRENCE FRAZIER, MBA POETRY BOOKS

AVAILABLE ON AMAZON

INTRODUCTION

WHY THIS BOOK EXISTS

Only 40% of American households have a budget.

Think about that number. Six out of ten families have no written plan for their money. They earn, they spend, they hope something is left over. Most months, nothing is.

This is not a book about theory. This is not a book written by someone who studied budgeting in a classroom and never lived it. I have spent 35 years as a lender and mortgage banker. I have seen thousands of people try to buy homes. I have watched families lose everything because they had no financial discipline. I have also watched families build wealth from nothing because they learned to control their money instead of letting their money control them.

The difference between the two groups is simple: one had a budget, one did not.

This book gives you a system. Not tips. Not suggestions. A system. The same system I have taught in seminars, on radio shows, in magazines, and in one-on-one consultations for over a decade. The system works if you work it. Most people will not work it. Most people will read this book, nod their heads, and change nothing. Those people will stay broke.

You are not most people. You picked up this book because something has to change. You are tired of living paycheck to paycheck. You are tired of debt. You are tired of watching everyone else build wealth while you tread water. You want to own a home. You want to retire with dignity. You want to leave something for your children.

Good. That means you are ready.

This book is for people who are serious about homeownership and wealth building. This book is for people who are willing to make sacrifices now for freedom later. This book is for people who understand that discipline is not restriction, discipline is power.

HERE IS HOW TO USE THIS BOOK

Read it once all the way through. Do not stop to take notes. Do not start making changes halfway through. Read the entire system first so you understand how all the pieces connect.

Then go back to Chapter 1 and start building your foundation. Write your mission statement. Write your vision statement. Set your SMART goals. Identify your accountability partner. Do not skip these steps. If you skip the foundation, the budget will not hold.

Then follow the system in order:

Start with Chapter 2 and complete the one-month audit. You need truth before you need tactics. When you know where your money is going, you stop guessing and start governing.

Next, go to Chapter 3 and build your Income Blueprint. A business cannot cut expenses into prosperity, and neither can a household. Income is the engine. You must learn how You,

Inc. generates, multiplies, and expands revenue before you attempt to perfect allocation.

Then implement the Allocation System in Chapter 4. This is where your income gets disciplined. This is where every dollar is assigned a job before it disappears. Allocation is how power becomes progress.

After allocation, move into Chapter 5 and cut expenses using the Elimination List. This is where you prune what is unnecessary so the essentials can grow. You are not "doing without." You are doing with purpose.

Then study Chapter 6 to avoid the mistakes that quietly destroy budgets over time. Many people create a plan and still fail because they repeat predictable patterns. This chapter helps you break them.

Finally, use Chapter 7 to choose tools, automate the system, and understand the wealth connection—how disciplined execution becomes homeownership, stability, investing, and legacy.

Follow the system in order. Do not pick and choose the parts you like. A budget is not inspiration—it is implementation.

This book works.

Let's begin.

CHAPTER 1
THE FOUNDATION – BEFORE YOU BUDGET

Most people jump straight into budgeting without building the one thing that makes budgeting work: a foundation. They want a spreadsheet to solve what is really a leadership problem. Budgets don't fail because people can't add. Budgets fail because people don't govern their money with clarity, consistency, and conviction.

Money is power—not because money is holy, but because money is functional. Money allows you to do things. It gives you options. It creates mobility. It buys time. It secures shelter. It pays for education. It protects your family in emergencies. In a capitalist society, money is one of the primary tools through which life is lived. Complaining about that reality does nothing. Accepting it—and learning how to operate inside it with wisdom—is the beginning of discipline.

This book is not about becoming obsessed with money. It's about refusing to be controlled by money. It's about turning your financial life from reaction into order. And before we touch a single budget category, I want you to adopt a different identity: you are not just a person trying to "manage bills." You are You, Inc. You are the CEO of your household economy. You make strategic decisions—or life makes them for you.

If you do not build a foundation first, any budget you create will be temporary. It will collapse under pressure, because pressure always reveals what was never truly established.

Biblical Foundations for Your Financial Life

Money is not just arithmetic. Money is spiritual.

If you believe God created you, equipped you, and sustains you, then the abilities you possess, the opportunities placed before you, and the income you earn are not accidents. They are assignments. You are the steward, not the owner.

Scripture calls this stewardship: God provides the resources; we manage the resources.

The parable of the talents illustrates this truth with striking clarity. The master gives different amounts to each servant. Two servants take what they were given, work, trade, risk, and multiply it. They are rewarded not because they started with more, but because they did more with what they were entrusted. The servant who buried his talent out of fear and neglect is rebuked—not for being poor, but for being unproductive.

That story is not merely about "spiritual gifts." It is also an economic parable. It teaches that work, diligence, creativity, and productive effort are not optional—they are expressions of obedience.

There are 3 spiritual laws at work in your financial life:

1. **The law of sowing and reaping**

You cannot expect a harvest in an arena where you refuse to sow.

2. **The law of stewardship**

Everything in your financial life begins with stewardship. Stewardship is not a religious word reserved for Sunday sermons. Stewardship is the universal law of responsibility: if something is placed in your hands, you are accountable for how you manage it.

Scripture speaks to this plainly when it teaches that faithfulness in what is small is the training ground for what is greater.[1] If you cannot govern a few hundred dollars with consistency, it will not matter if you earn a few thousand more—because increased income without increased governance simply produces a higher-cost lifestyle.

Stewardship means your earning, spending, saving, and giving must operate under principles—not moods. It means you stop treating money as something that happens to you, and you begin treating it as something you direct. In business, we call that management. In life, we call it maturity. In theology, we call it stewardship.

This is why the foundation matters. God does not bless chaos. He blesses order. And order begins with a clear system —one that reflects who you are, what you believe, and where you are going.

3. **The law of alignment**

Your spending, earning, saving, and giving must align with your assignment. Disorder produces lack; alignment produces clarity and flow.

Many people pray for financial blessings while ignoring the principles God has already given: discipline, prudence, planning, integrity, generosity, and consistency. Prayer does not override neglect. Miracles do not cancel disorder. Faith is not an escape from responsibility—it is the power to fulfill responsibility.

This book is not just a budgeting guide. It is an invitation to honor God with how you manage the resources entrusted to you. When you track your spending, allocate your income, increase your earning capacity, pay down debt, and build reserves, you are participating in the ancient work of stewardship.

Budgeting becomes more than a financial tool.

It becomes a form of worship, a way of saying:

> "Everything I have comes from God. I will manage it with excellence. I will not bury my talent. I will multiply it for the sake of my family, my community, and the purpose God has assigned to my life."

This is the spiritual foundation of Run Your Household Like a Business.

Your Financial Why: The Mission Statement

Every successful organization has a mission statement. The mission statement answers one question: Why do we exist?

Businesses have mission statements. Apple exists to think differently and make technology accessible. Tesla exists to accelerate the transition to sustainable energy. Amazon exists to be the most customer-centric company on Earth. These mission statements guide every decision these companies make. When Apple decides whether to launch a product, they ask: Does this align with our mission? If yes, they proceed. If no, they do not. The mission statement is the filter for all choices.

You need a personal financial mission statement. Your mission statement answers: Why does my financial life exist? What is the purpose of earning money, saving money, and building wealth? What am I working toward? What matters most to me financially?

Most people have never asked themselves these questions. They earn money because they need to survive. They spend money because they want things. They have no deeper purpose. They have no mission. Without a mission, every spending decision becomes random. Without a mission, you cannot distinguish between important expenses and unimportant expenses. Without a mission, your budget has no direction.

Your mission statement becomes your North Star. Every financial decision gets filtered through your mission. Someone offers you a great deal on something you do not need? Check your mission. Does buying this align with why your financial life exists? No? Do not buy it. Your friends pressure you to go on an expensive vacation? Check your mission. Does this move you toward your financial purpose or away from it? Away? Decline. Your mission keeps you on track when emotions and outside pressure try to derail you.

Here is how to create your mission statement:

Sit down with a blank piece of paper. No phone. No distractions. Just you and the paper. Write at the top: Why does my financial life exist? Then start writing. Do not edit. Do not judge. Just write whatever comes to mind. Write for ten minutes without stopping.

Your answers might include things like: I want to provide for my family. I want to retire early. I want financial freedom. I want to never worry about money again. I want to leave an inheritance for my children. I want to buy a house. I want to travel the world. I want to start a business. I want to give generously to causes I care about. I want security. I want options. I want peace of mind.

All of these are valid. None is better than another. Your mission is your mission. Not someone else's mission. Your financial purpose comes from your values, your experiences, your fears, your dreams. Be honest. Write what matters to you, not what you think should matter.

After you write for ten minutes, read what you wrote. Look for themes. Look for the ideas that showed up multiple times. Look for the statements that triggered the strongest emotion when you wrote them. Those are your core financial motivations.

Now distill everything into one or two sentences. This is your personal financial mission statement. It should be specific enough to guide decisions but broad enough to cover your major financial goals. It should inspire you. It should remind you why you are making sacrifices now for benefits later.

Here are examples of strong mission statements:

> "My financial mission is to build enough wealth to retire by age fifty so I can spend my later years traveling and serving my community instead of working for money."
>
> "My financial mission is to provide a stable, secure life for my family and to break the cycle of poverty that has defined my family for generations."
>
> "My financial mission is to achieve complete financial independence so I never have to make career decisions based on money and can instead pursue work I find meaningful."
>
> "My financial mission is to build wealth that allows me to be generous with those in need and to fund causes that matter to me without worrying about my own financial security."
>
> "My financial mission is to own my home outright and to never carry debt again so I can live with complete financial peace."

Notice these mission statements are personal. They reflect individual values and goals. They are not generic. They are specific to the person who wrote them. Your mission statement should be equally personal and specific to you.

Write your mission statement today. Right now. Stop reading. Get paper. Write for ten minutes. Distill into one or two sentences. Do not move forward until you have a mission statement you believe in.

Once you have your mission statement, write it somewhere you will see it daily. Put it on your bathroom mirror. Put it on your refrigerator. Put it as the wallpaper on your phone. Make it impossible to ignore. You need to see your mission every single day. When you face a difficult financial choice, read your mission. Ask yourself: Does this choice align with my mission or contradict it? Then choose accordingly.

Your mission statement is your financial constitution. Everything else flows from this. The mission gives your budget purpose. The mission gives your sacrifices meaning. The mission reminds you why you are doing this when the process gets hard.

Your Financial Destination: The Vision Statement

Your mission statement explains why your financial life exists. Your vision statement describes where your financial life is going. The mission is your purpose. The vision is your destination.

A vision statement paints a picture of your future. Not just what you want to have, but who you want to be. Not just goals, but identity. Your vision describes your life five, ten, or twenty years from now after you have achieved your financial mission. Your vision is the movie you play in your head that keeps you motivated when budgeting feels restrictive.

Most people have vague financial visions. They want to be rich. They want to be comfortable. They want to not worry about money. These visions are too abstract. You cannot work toward an abstract concept. You need specificity. You need detail. You need clarity.

Here is how to create your vision statement.

Close your eyes. Imagine your life ten years from now. You have achieved your financial mission. You have built the wealth you wanted. You have the financial freedom you worked toward. What does your life look like?

Where do you live? Do you own your home? What does it look like? What neighborhood? What city? Who lives with you? What does your daily routine look like? What time do you wake up? What do you do with your days? Are you still working? If yes, what kind of work? If no, how do you spend your time? What hobbies do you pursue? What relationships do you prioritize? How do you serve others? How do you give back? What does a typical weekend look like? What does vacation look like? How do you feel emotionally? How do you feel about money? What stresses have disappeared? What new opportunities have appeared?

Get specific. Paint the picture in as much detail as possible. The more vivid the vision, the more motivating it becomes. Generic visions do not inspire. Specific visions pull you forward.

Write your vision statement as if you are writing from the future. Use present tense. Describe your life as if you are already living it.

Here is an example of a strong vision statement:

"Ten years from now, I own my three-bedroom home

in a quiet neighborhood outside the city. The mortgage is paid off. I wake up every morning without an alarm. I work part-time doing consulting work I find interesting, but I only work because I want to, not because I need to. My kids' college funds are fully funded. My retirement accounts are on track to support me comfortably into my eighties. I have six months of expenses in my emergency fund, which gives me complete peace of mind. I volunteer three days per week at the local community center teaching financial literacy to people who are where I used to be. I take my family on a two-week vacation every summer without worrying about cost. My marriage is strong because money is no longer a source of conflict. I sleep peacefully every night knowing I am financially secure. I feel proud of what I built. I feel free."

This vision is specific. You can see it. You can feel it. You can taste it. This person knows exactly what they are working toward. When this person is tempted to overspend, they think about the vision. They ask: Does buying this move me toward my vision or away from it? The answer is usually obvious. The vision guides the decision.

Write your vision statement. Make it detailed. Make it emotional. Make it real. This is the future you are building with every dollar you save, every expense you cut, every budget decision you make correctly.

Once you have your vision, read it every week. Sunday night is a good time. Read your vision before you start a new week of budgeting. Remind yourself where you are going. Let the vision motivate you to make good choices in the coming week. Let the vision sustain you when budgeting feels hard.

Your vision statement works with your mission statement. The mission is why you do this. The vision is what this creates. Together, they give your budget both purpose and direction. You are not just restricting spending. You are building a specific future. That makes all the difference.

Your Financial Targets: SMART Goals

Your mission statement gives you purpose. Your vision statement gives you direction. Now you need specific targets. These are your goals.

Most people set terrible goals. They say things like: "I want to save more money." "I want to pay off debt." "I want to be financially secure." These are not goals. These are wishes. Wishes do not create results. Goals create results.

A goal must be SMART. This is an acronym. SMART stands for Specific, Measurable, Achievable, Relevant, and Time-bound. Every goal you set must meet all five criteria or it is not a real goal.

Specific means you know exactly what you are trying to accomplish. Not "save more money" but "save ten thousand dollars." Not "pay off debt" but "pay off my car loan." Not "be financially secure" but "build a six-month emergency fund." Vague goals produce vague results. Specific goals produce specific results.

Measurable means you can track your progress. You know when you are fifty percent done. You know when you are seventy-five percent done. You know exactly when you achieved the goal. If you cannot measure it, you cannot manage it. Your goal must have numbers attached. Dollars. Months. Percentages. Something you can track.

Achievable means the goal is possible given your current situation. You make three thousand dollars per month. You want to save ten thousand dollars this year. The math works. You can do this if you budget well and cut expenses. The goal is challenging but not impossible. Goals that are too easy do not motivate. Goals that are impossible create discouragement. Find the sweet spot. Challenging but achievable.

Relevant means the goal aligns with your mission and vision. The goal moves you toward your financial purpose. The goal fits into your bigger picture. Do not set goals just because other people say you should. Set goals that matter to you based on your mission and vision. If your mission is to retire early, then saving for retirement is a relevant goal. If your mission is to buy a house, then building a down payment fund is a relevant goal. Every goal must connect to your why.

Time-bound means the goal has a deadline. Not "someday I will save ten thousand dollars" but "I will save ten thousand dollars by December 31st of this year." Deadlines create urgency. Deadlines force action. Without a deadline, goals drift forever into the future. With a deadline, you must act now. Set specific dates. Put them on your calendar. Hold yourself accountable to those dates.

Here are examples of SMART goals versus non-SMART goals:

Non-SMART: "I want to save money."

SMART: "I will save five thousand dollars for an emergency fund by June 30th, 2026 by saving four hundred seventeen dollars per month."

Non-SMART: "I want to get out of debt."

SMART: "I will pay off my fifteen thousand dollar car loan by December 31st, 2026 by paying one thousand two hundred fifty dollars per month using the debt snowball method."

Non-SMART: "I want to buy a house someday."

SMART: "I will save twenty thousand dollars for a house down payment by December 31st, 2027 by saving six hundred sixty-seven dollars per month and working a part-time job on weekends to generate extra income."

Non-SMART: "I want to be financially secure."

SMART: "I will build a six-month emergency fund totaling eighteen thousand dollars by December 31st, 2028 by saving three hundred seventy-five dollars per month for four years."

See the difference? SMART goals are concrete. You can visualize achieving them. You can track your progress. You know exactly what to do each month. Non-SMART goals are fog. You cannot grab fog. You cannot measure fog. SMART goals are solid targets you can aim at and hit.

You need three types of SMART goals: short-term goals (achieve within one year), medium-term goals (achieve within one to five years), and long-term goals (achieve within five to ten years or more).

Short-term goals keep you motivated because you see progress quickly. Examples: save one thousand dollar starter emergency fund, pay off smallest credit card, save for holiday spending, build one month of expenses in savings.

Medium-term goals require sustained effort over several years. Examples: pay off car loan, save house down payment, build full six-month emergency fund, pay off all consumer debt except mortgage.

Long-term goals shape your overall financial trajectory. Examples: pay off mortgage, save for retirement, achieve financial independence, build generational wealth to pass to children.

Write one short-term goal, two medium-term goals, and one long-term goal right now. Make them SMART. Make them specific. Make them measurable. Make them achievable. Make them relevant to your mission and vision. Make them time-bound with actual dates.

Once you have your goals written, break them down into monthly action steps. Your short-term goal is to save five thousand dollars in twelve months. That is four hundred seventeen dollars per month. Write that down. Put it in your budget. That monthly number is what you track. That monthly number is what you hold yourself accountable to hitting.

Your medium-term goal is to pay off fifteen thousand in car loan debt in eighteen months. That is eight hundred thirty-three dollars per month. Write that down. Put it in your budget. Track it monthly. Adjust if you fall behind. Celebrate when you stay on pace.

Breaking goals into monthly targets makes them manageable. Saving five thousand dollars feels overwhelming. Saving four hundred seventeen dollars this month feels doable. You can find four hundred seventeen dollars. You can cut expenses. You can work extra hours. You can make it happen this month. Then you do it again next month. Twelve times, and you hit your goal. Monthly targets turn impossible-feeling goals into a series of achievable steps.

Review your goals monthly. Are you on track? If yes, keep going. If no, figure out why. Did you overestimate your income? Did you underestimate your expenses? Did something unexpected happen? Adjust your timeline or adjust your budget. But do not abandon the goal. Adjust and continue. Progress, not perfection.

Your SMART goals transform your abstract mission and vision into concrete action plans. The mission is why. The vision is where. The goals are what, when, and how much. Together, these three elements create unstoppable forward momentum toward the financial future you want.

Your Personal Business Plan: Running You, Inc.

Here is what most people miss about budgeting: a household is an economy. It is not just a place where people live—it is a system that produces income, makes decisions, manages resources, absorbs shocks, and attempts to build a future. That is a business whether you call it that or not.

You are an entity, a corporation.

In business, you do not start by arguing over the office supply budget. You start with the revenue plan. You ask: how will we generate income consistently? How will we protect that income against disruption? How will we increase it over time? And only then do you design spending, savings, staffing, and cost discipline.

Households must be led the same way. Income sets the boundary for what is possible. If a family wants a $1 million home but earns $25,000 a year, the issue is not budgeting—the issue is revenue. The dream is constrained by income. So the correct question becomes: what skills, credentials, positioning, career moves, side income, or business creation must occur for that goal to become reasonable?

This is why this book starts with foundation before budget. The budget is not the beginning. The budget is the execution tool for a larger plan. And the larger plan requires leadership.

Long-Term Financial Projections

Every business creates projections for three years, five years, seven years, and ten years into the future. These projections answer: Where will we be financially at each milestone? How much revenue will we generate? What will our assets look like? What will our net worth be? These projections guide current decisions because the business knows where it needs to be in the future.

You need the same projections for You. Where will you be financially in three years? What will your income be? What will your savings balance be? What debt will be eliminated? What assets will you own? Create specific dollar amounts and dates for each milestone.

In three years, I will have zero consumer debt, fifteen thousand dollars in emergency savings, and fifty thousand dollars in retirement accounts. That is a projection. Now you know what you are working toward. Now you can work backward to figure out what you need to do monthly to hit those numbers.

In five years, I will own my home with a mortgage balance fifty thousand dollars less than today, have twenty-five thousand in emergency savings, and one hundred twenty thousand in retirement accounts. That is a projection. Again, work backward. What must you do each month for five years to make this real?

In seven years, I will have paid off my mortgage completely, have forty thousand in liquid savings, have two hundred thousand in retirement accounts, and have started investing in real estate through a rental property that generates five hundred dollars monthly passive income. That is a projection. More detailed. More ambitious. Still achievable if you plan correctly.

In ten years, I will have a net worth of five hundred thousand dollars, generate two thousand dollars monthly in passive income from investments, work part-time because I want to rather than because I have to, and have complete financial freedom to make life decisions without money being the primary consideration. That is a projection. This is the ten-year target. Everything you do today moves you toward this target or away from it.

Write your projections today. Be specific. Use real numbers. Push yourself to be ambitious but realistic. These projections become the milestones that keep you motivated over the long years of disciplined budgeting. When you are tired of living lean, you look at your seven-year projection and remember why you are doing this. The projection pulls you forward.

The Revenue Plan – How You, Inc. Generates Power

Every successful business begins with a simple but decisive question:

How will we generate revenue—consistently, sustainably, and at a level that supports our mission?

Boards of directors do not start by discussing the office supply budget. They start with revenue, sales, and growth. Without a revenue plan, there is no business plan. Without income, there is nothing to manage.

Mark Cuban has said it plainly: "Sales cures all."

If a business knows how to generate revenue, it can recover from mistakes, survive downturns, and grow. If it cannot generate revenue, nothing else matters.

Your household is no different.

Your family is not just a collection of people sharing expenses. It is an enterprise—an economic unit with goals, responsibilities, and a future. Every enterprise must have a revenue plan. Without adequate income, your capacity is limited no matter how disciplined your budgeting becomes.

A budget allocates power.
Income creates power.

If your dream is to own a $1,000,000 home, and that realistically requires a $250,000 annual income, but you currently earn $25,000, then the issue is not simply overspending—it is under-earning. No budgeting app can compensate for a structural income gap that large. The dream is not wrong; the strategy is incomplete.

The question for You, Inc. is therefore a business question:

- What is your current annual revenue?
- What revenue level does your mission require?
- What skills, training, certifications, or strategic moves must you pursue to close the gap?
- If you are in sales, how will you improve your client base, system, and value proposition?
- If you are in operations, how will you position yourself for roles that match your capability and contribution?
- What additional revenue streams can stabilize your household during economic fluctuations?

Companies invest in R&D to create new products.

Families invest in education and skill development for the same reason.

Companies invest in marketing and sales to expand revenue.

Families invest in networking, entrepreneurship, and career advancement.

Companies diversify income streams to survive downturns.

Families must do the same to protect long-term stability.

Your income is not a fixed outcome.

It is a design project.

The Power Budget will help you allocate your money, eliminate waste, and build stability. But income is what makes all of that scalable. If you are serious about owning a home, building wealth, and leaving a legacy, you must be just as serious about increasing your earning power as you are about controlling expenses.

From this point forward, adopt the mindset of a CEO:

"I am increasing my capacity. I am expanding my revenue. I am multiplying what God placed in my hands."

That is what wise stewards do.
That is what You, Inc. must do.

Capital Plan: Your Starting Funds

Every business needs starting capital. This is the money required to begin operations and survive until the business becomes profitable. A restaurant needs capital for equipment, inventory, and several months of operating expenses before it makes its first dollar. A software company needs capital for development costs, marketing, and runway before generating revenue. No business succeeds without adequate starting capital.

You, Inc. needs starting capital too. Your starting capital is your emergency fund. This is not optional. This is not something you build after you feel comfortable. This is the money you must have before you can operate your personal finances successfully.

Your starter emergency fund is one thousand to two thousand dollars. This covers small unexpected expenses so they do not derail your budget. Car repair, medical bill, appliance breakdown. These things happen. Without starting capital, they destroy your budget and force you into debt. With starting capital, they are inconveniences you handle and move past. Build this starter fund first before working on any other goal.

Your full capital requirement is six to twelve months of

expenses. This is your complete emergency fund. This protects You, Inc. from catastrophic events. Job loss, major medical emergency, extended car repairs, significant home repairs. These events require serious capital to survive. Most people have no capital. When catastrophe strikes, they collapse financially. They lose everything. They declare bankruptcy. They never recover.

You will have capital. You will build the full emergency fund over time. First you save the starter fund of one to two thousand. Then you attack debt. Then you build the full fund of six to twelve months. This might take three to five years. That is acceptable. The important thing is you build it. You protect You, Inc. from failure. You ensure your business can survive anything.

Businesses that operate without adequate capital reserves fail at high rates. Personal finances that operate without emergency funds fail at high rates. The pattern is identical. Capital is not optional. Capital is the difference between surviving setbacks and being destroyed by setbacks. Build your capital. Protect your business.

Operational Plan: Your Monthly Budget

Every business has an operational plan. This document details exactly how the business runs day to day. How much money comes in. How much goes out. What each department spends. What the profit margins are. How resources are allocated. The operational plan is reviewed regularly and adjusted based on actual results versus projections.

Your operational plan is your monthly budget. This is not a restrictive document that ruins your fun. This is a professional operations manual for running You, Inc. successfully. Your operational plan tells you exactly how much money comes in each month, exactly where every dollar goes, and exactly how much you save and invest.

Chapter 3 of this book teaches you the allocation system that becomes your operational plan. You will allocate percentages of your income to high priority expenses, medium priority expenses, low priority expenses, emergency savings, and debt elimination. These allocations are your operating procedures. Follow them and You, Inc. runs profitably. Ignore them and You, Inc. runs at a loss and eventually fails.

Your operational plan must be reviewed weekly at minimum. Every Sunday evening, review last week's spending. Compare actual spending to planned spending in each category. Identify variances. Understand why they occurred. Adjust behavior for the coming week. This weekly review is the equivalent of a business reviewing its P&L statement. Businesses that do not review financial performance regularly make bad decisions and waste resources. You will review weekly. You will make good decisions. You will conserve resources.

Your operational plan must be updated monthly. At the end of each month, you reconcile your entire budget. Did you stay within limits in every category? Where did you overspend? Where did you underspend? What unexpected expenses occurred? What should you budget differently next month? You adjust. You improve. You optimize your operations month after month.

Businesses treat their operational plans as sacred documents. They follow them religiously. They measure everything. They hold people accountable to the plan. You will treat your budget the same way. Your budget is not a suggestion. Your budget is your operational manual. You follow it. You measure your performance against it. You hold yourself accountable to it. This is how successful businesses operate. This is how You, Inc. will operate.

Reserves Goal: Your Emergency Fund Target

We already discussed capital and emergency funds, but let me emphasize this again in business terms. Every responsible business maintains reserves. These reserves are not for normal operations. Operational funds come from revenue. Reserves are for when something goes wrong. Economic downturn. Major client lost. Unexpected lawsuit. Equipment failure. Disasters that threaten the business's survival.

Companies that maintain adequate reserves survive disasters. Companies without reserves fail when disasters strike. This is not opinion. This is observable fact across every industry and every economic cycle.

Your reserves goal is your fully funded emergency fund. The target is six to twelve months of expenses. For someone spending three thousand per month, that is eighteen thousand to thirty-six thousand dollars sitting in a separate savings account earning interest but otherwise untouched. This feels like a lot of money. It feels wasteful to have this money sitting instead of being invested or used to pay off debt faster.

This feeling is wrong. Reserves are never wasted. Reserves are insurance. You hope you never need them. You are grateful they exist when you do need them. Reserves are what allow you to weather storms without destroying your financial progress. Reserves are what prevent you from going back into debt when unexpected expenses hit. Reserves are what give you peace of mind and financial stability.

Build your reserves methodically. After you save your starter emergency fund and pay off all non-mortgage debt, you attack the reserves goal. You redirect all the money you were paying toward debt into building your full emergency fund. You save three hundred seventy-five dollars per month for four years and you have eighteen thousand. You save six hundred twenty-five per month for four years and you have thirty thousand. Pick your target. Work toward it relentlessly. Do not stop until you hit full funding.

Once your reserves are fully funded, you can finally shift focus completely to wealth building through investments and paying off your mortgage. But not before. Reserves come first. Stability comes before growth. Protection comes before optimization. This is sound business practice. This is how You, Inc. achieves lasting success.

Bookkeeping System: Tracking Every Dollar

Every business tracks every dollar that comes in and goes out. Revenue is recorded. Expenses are categorized. Receipts are saved. Bank statements are reconciled. Financial reports are generated monthly. The bookkeeping system is not optional. The bookkeeping system is how the business knows if it is profitable, where money is being wasted, and whether the operational plan is working.

Businesses that do not maintain accurate books fail quickly. They run out of money and do not know why. They think they are profitable when they are losing money. They make bad decisions based on bad information. They collapse.

You need a bookkeeping system for You, Inc. This is your spending tracking from Chapter 2 and your budgeting software from Chapter 7. Every dollar you earn gets recorded. Every dollar you spend gets categorized. Every transaction gets reviewed. Your bank accounts get reconciled monthly. You know exactly where you stand financially at all times.

Your bookkeeping system has two phases. Phase one is the one-month audit from Chapter 2. This is discovery. You track every expense for thirty days to understand your current spending patterns. You categorize everything. You identify waste. You see reality. This audit becomes the foundation for your budget. You cannot build a budget without knowing where money currently goes. The audit is your baseline financial report.

Phase two is ongoing tracking after your budget is created. You track every expense daily. You compare actual spending to budgeted amounts. You use a budgeting app that automatically pulls transactions from your linked bank accounts, or you manually enter every transaction into a spreadsheet. Either way, you track consistently. You review daily. You reconcile monthly. Your bookkeeping system runs continuously.

Most people hate tracking. They think it is tedious. They think it takes too much time. They think they can skip this step. Those people fail at budgeting. You cannot manage what you do not measure. You cannot improve what you do not track. Businesses know this. You know this now too. You will track every dollar because tracking is the only way to know if your operational plan is working.

Your bookkeeping system also includes maintaining financial records. Keep bank statements for at least one year. Keep tax returns for at least seven years. Keep receipts for major purchases. Keep documentation for insurance claims. Organize your files. Know where everything is. Businesses maintain records because records protect them legally and provide historical data for decision-making. You maintain records for the same reasons. You are running a business. Act like it.

Mission and Vision: Your Business Purpose and Direction

Before you budget, you need to know what you're building. Budgeting without purpose becomes punishment. Budgeting with purpose becomes power.

Set aside time and do this with intention—no phone, no distractions, no multitasking. Take a blank sheet of paper and write three things: your mission, your vision, and your goals. This is not corporate theater. This is personal clarity.

Your mission statement answers: Why does my financial life matter?

It is your purpose. It is your "why." It should be short, direct, and personal. For example:

"My mission is to build a stable household economy that supports homeownership, eliminates debt, and creates long-term generational security."

Your vision statement answers: What does success look like?

It paints a clear picture of the future. It is where you are headed, not what you are doing today. For example:

"My vision is to own a home, maintain a six-month reserve, invest consistently, and create assets that produce income beyond my labor."

Now turn that purpose into measurable targets using SMART goals. SMART goals are not motivational quotes; they are operational commitments.

- Specific: clear outcome
- Measurable: a number, a target, a finish line
- Achievable: realistic based on income and time
- Relevant: connected to your mission and vision
- Time-bound: a deadline, not "someday"

A weak goal sounds like: "I want to buy a house someday."

A strong goal sounds like: "I will purchase a home by December 31, 2027 by saving $___ for down payment and reserves, improving my credit profile, and maintaining a fixed monthly surplus of $___."

Notice what a real goal does: it forces you to confront income reality and expense behavior honestly. It turns hope into a plan.

Core Values: Your Operating Principles

Every strong business has core values. These are the principles that guide behavior and decisions. Honesty. Integrity. Excellence. Customer focus. Innovation. These values are not just words on a wall. These values determine how the business operates when nobody is watching. These values shape culture and define what the business will and will not do.

You need core values for You, Inc. These are the financial principles you will not violate no matter what. These values guide your budget decisions when emotions run high or when outside pressure mounts. These values are your lines in the sand.

Here are examples of strong financial core values:

"I value long-term financial security over short-term pleasure."

This core value means you do not impulse buy. You do not go into debt for things you want but do not need. You prioritize saving and investing over spending on temporary enjoyment. When you are tempted to splurge, you remember this core value. You ask: Does this align with valuing long-term security over short-term pleasure? The answer is no. You do not buy.

"I value financial independence over material possessions."

This core value means you care more about being debt-free and having savings than you care about having the newest car, the biggest house, or the nicest clothes. You choose to live below your means. You accumulate wealth, not stuff. When someone judges your old car or modest home, you remember this core value. Their opinion is irrelevant. Your values are different. You are building independence while they are building debt.

"I value experiences with loved ones over accumulating things."

This core value means you spend money on family trips, dinners with friends, and creating memories rather than buying more possessions that clutter your home and your life. You say no to shopping and yes to relationships. When you are tempted to buy something you do not need, you remember this core value. That money could create an experience with someone you love instead. You redirect the money toward what matters.

"I value transparency and honesty in all financial dealings."

This core value means you do not hide purchases from your spouse. You do not lie about money. You do not cheat on taxes. You do not take advantage of people financially. You operate with integrity even when you could get away with dishonesty. Your character matters more than short-term gain. This core value builds trust in relationships and keeps you out of legal and moral trouble.

"I value generosity and helping others while maintaining my own financial stability."

This core value means you give to people in need and support causes you care about, but you do so from a position of strength, not from a position of weakness. You do not sacrifice your own financial stability to help others. You build your emergency fund and eliminate your debt first. Then you give generously from your overflow. You help more people over the long term by building wealth first and giving consistently rather than giving impulsively and staying broke.

Choose three to five core values for You, Inc. Write them down. These values must be true reflections of what matters to you, not what you think should matter. If you write core values you do not actually believe, they will not guide your behavior. Be honest. Write values that resonate with who you are and who you want to become.

Once you have your core values written, review them monthly. Are you living according to your values? Did any financial decision this month violate your core values? If yes, why? What will you do differently? Core values only work if you actually use them to guide decisions. Check yourself regularly. Stay aligned.

Belief Statement: Your Financial Philosophy

Your core values are the principles you operate by. Your belief statement is different. Your belief statement is what you fundamentally believe about money, wealth, and financial success. This is your philosophy. This is your worldview. This is the lens through which you see all financial matters.

Businesses have belief statements even if they do not call them that. Companies believe certain things about markets, customers, competition, and success. These beliefs shape strategy. A company that believes markets are efficient behaves differently than a company that believes markets are inefficient. A company that believes customers are rational behaves differently than a company that believes customers are emotional. Beliefs drive behavior.

You have financial beliefs whether you have articulated them or not. These beliefs determine how you make money decisions. If you believe money is scarce and hard to get, you hoard what you have and never feel secure no matter how much you save. If you believe money flows easily to those who work hard, you focus on earning more rather than worrying about losing what you have. If you believe debt is normal and unavoidable, you accept car payments and credit card balances as facts of life. If you believe debt is a choice and a trap, you avoid it aggressively and work to eliminate it.

Your current financial results reflect your current financial beliefs. If you are broke and in debt, you have beliefs that lead to being broke and in debt. If you want different results, you need different beliefs. You need to identify your current beliefs, evaluate whether they serve you, and replace limiting beliefs with empowering beliefs.

Here is how to create your belief statement. Answer these questions honestly:

What do I believe about money? Is it scarce or abundant? Is it good or evil? Is it a tool or a goal? Is it something I control or something that controls me?

What do I believe about wealth? Is it achievable for someone like me or only for other people? Is it earned through hard work or through luck? Is it moral or immoral to want wealth?

What do I believe about debt? Is it a normal part of life or something to avoid? Is it a tool to build wealth or a trap that destroys wealth? Is it shameful to have debt or is everyone in debt?

What do I believe about my ability to succeed financially? Do I believe I can learn to budget and build wealth or do I believe I am bad with money and always will be? Do I believe my current situation is permanent or temporary? Do I believe change is possible?

Write your answers. Look at what you wrote. These are your current beliefs. Some of these beliefs are probably helping you. Some are probably hurting you.

Now write your new belief statement. This is what you choose to believe going forward. These are the beliefs that will guide You, Inc. to success.

Here are examples of powerful belief statements:

"I believe anyone can build wealth regardless of starting point if they have discipline and a plan. I believe my current financial situation is temporary and completely within my power to change. I believe money is a tool for creating security and opportunities, not a measure of my worth as a person. I believe debt is a choice, not a necessity, and I choose to eliminate it from my life. I believe living below my means today creates freedom tomorrow. I believe I am fully capable of learning to budget, saving consistently, and building lasting wealth."

"I believe wealth is not about how much you earn but about how much you keep and grow. I believe most people stay broke because they lack discipline and a plan, not because they lack income. I believe I can earn more money by increasing my skills and working strategically. I believe frugality is not deprivation but wisdom. I believe delayed gratification leads to greater long-term satisfaction than instant gratification. I believe I control my financial destiny through the choices I make daily."

"I believe money is abundant and flows to those who provide value to others. I believe I become wealthy by solving problems and serving people, not by hoarding or manipulating. I believe generosity and wealth building are compatible when done from a position of financial strength. I believe financial education is more valuable than formal education for building wealth. I believe most financial advice is designed to make someone else rich, so I will educate myself and make my own decisions. I believe I am the CEO of my financial life and nobody cares about my success more than I do."

Write your belief statement. Make it personal. Make it powerful. Make it true for you. This statement becomes the foundation of how You, Inc. operates. When you face difficult financial decisions, you come back to your beliefs. What does someone with my beliefs do in this situation? Then you act accordingly.

Your beliefs shape your thoughts. Your thoughts shape your actions. Your actions shape your results. Change your beliefs, change your results. Write a belief statement that empowers you to build the wealth you want.

PUTTING YOUR PERSONAL BUSINESS PLAN TOGETHER

You now have all the components of a comprehensive personal business plan for You, Inc. Let me summarize what you have built:

Long-term projections: You know where you are going financially in three, five, seven, and ten years. You have specific targets. You are working backward from those targets to determine what you must do today.

Revenue plan: You understand that income is not fixed—it is a design project. You know your current revenue and the revenue level your mission requires. You are committed to increasing your earning capacity strategically.

Capital plan: You are building your emergency fund as starting capital. You know you need one to two thousand for a starter fund and six to twelve months of expenses for a full fund. Capital protects You, Inc. from failure.

Operational plan: You are creating a monthly budget that allocates every dollar strategically. Your operational plan guides day-to-day spending decisions and ensures You, Inc. runs profitably.

Reserves goal: You have a clear target for your emergency fund. You know this is not optional. Reserves are what allow You, Inc. to survive disasters and continue operations during difficult times.

Bookkeeping system: You track every dollar through the one-month audit and ongoing spending tracking. You use budgeting software or spreadsheets. You reconcile monthly. You know your numbers at all times.

Mission statement: You know why your financial life exists. Your mission guides all decisions and keeps you focused on what matters most.

Vision statement: You know what your financial future

looks like in vivid detail. Your vision motivates you to make sacrifices now for benefits later.

SMART goals: You have specific, measurable, achievable, relevant, time-bound targets for the short term, medium term, and long term. Your goals break your vision into actionable steps.

Core values: You have three to five principles that guide your financial behavior. Your values are your lines in the sand. You make decisions based on values, not emotions or outside pressure.

Belief statement: You have articulated what you believe about money, wealth, debt, and your ability to succeed. Your beliefs empower you to take the actions necessary to build wealth.

This is your complete personal business plan. This is the foundation that makes your budget unbreakable. This is what most people skip and why most people fail. You did not skip it. You built it. You are ready to succeed.

YOUR ACCOUNTABILITY PARTNER: THE BOARD OF DIRECTORS

Every business has a board of directors. The board holds leadership accountable. The board asks hard questions. The board provides guidance and perspective. The board does not let the CEO make excuses or drift off course. The board ensures the business stays on mission and moves toward its vision.

You need a board of directors for You, Inc. In practical terms, this means you need an accountability partner. One person who knows your mission, your vision, your goals, your values, and your beliefs. One person who tracks your progress with you. One person who calls you out when you break your budget. One person who celebrates with you when you hit milestones. One person who will not let you quit.

Your accountability partner must meet specific criteria. They must care about your success. They must be financially responsible themselves. They must be willing to have difficult conversations with you. They must be someone you respect enough that their opinion matters. They must agree to the role and commit to regular check-ins.

Your accountability partner is not your parent, your spouse, or your best friend unless that person meets the criteria above. Many people choose a spouse as an accountability partner. This works if the spouse is financially disciplined and you can have honest conversations without conflict. This fails if money is a source of tension in your relationship or if one person is not committed to the budget.

Some people choose a friend who is also budgeting. You become accountability partners for each other. You compare notes. You share struggles. You encourage each other. This works well because you are going through the same journey simultaneously.

Some people choose a financial coach or counselor. You pay someone to hold you accountable. This works if you need more structure and expertise. Professional accountability partners keep you on track and provide education along the way.

Whoever you choose, make the arrangement formal. Tell them: "I am working on building wealth through disciplined budgeting. I need someone to hold me accountable. Will you be my accountability partner?" Explain what that means. Weekly or monthly check-ins. Sharing your budget and spending reports. Permission to ask hard questions and give honest feedback. Celebrating wins together.

Once you have an accountability partner, schedule your check-ins. Weekly is ideal for the first three months while you are building new habits. Monthly is sufficient after that for most people. Stick to the schedule. Do not skip check-ins. The check-ins are what keep you honest.

What do you discuss in check-ins? Review your budget. Did you stay within spending limits in every category? If no, what happened? What will you do differently? Review your goals. Are you on pace to hit your targets? If no, what needs to change? Discuss challenges. What temptations did you face? How did you handle them? What decisions are you struggling with? Get input. Celebrate progress. Did you hit a milestone? Pay off a debt? Reach a savings target? Acknowledge success. These wins fuel motivation.

Your accountability partner is not there to judge you or control you. Your accountability partner is there to support you and keep you honest. There will be months you fail. You will overspend. You will break your budget. Your accountability partner does not shame you. They help you understand what went wrong, make a plan to fix it, and move forward. This is grace combined with honesty. This is what you need.

Most people try to budget alone. They tell nobody about their goals. They keep their struggles private. They have nobody to report to. When they fail, nobody knows. When they quit, nobody holds them accountable. They drift back to old patterns. Nothing changes.

You will not budget alone. You will have an accountability partner. You will share your plan. You will report your progress. You will accept feedback. You will stay on track because someone is watching and someone cares. This is the difference between trying and succeeding.

YOUR ASSIGNMENT FOR THIS CHAPTER

Do not move to Chapter 2 until you complete this assignment. Everything in this book builds on the foundation you create in this chapter. Skip this foundation and everything else crumbles.

Here is what you must do:

Write your personal financial mission statement. Spend ten minutes writing why your financial life exists. Distill it into one or two powerful sentences. Put it somewhere you will see it daily.

Write your vision statement. Describe your life ten years from now in vivid detail. What does success look like? Who are you? How do you live? What have you achieved? Write as if you are already living that life.

Create your SMART goals. Write one short-term goal, two medium-term goals, and one long-term goal. Make them specific, measurable, achievable, relevant, and time-bound. Break each goal into monthly action steps.

Write your long-term financial projections. Where will you be in three years, five years, seven years, and ten years? Use specific dollar amounts for income, savings, debt levels, and net worth.

Create your revenue plan. What is your current annual income? What income level does your mission require? What specific actions will you take to increase your earning capacity? Write a concrete plan.

Identify your core values. Choose three to five financial principles that will guide your decisions. Write them down. Commit to living by them.

Write your belief statement. What do you believe about money, wealth, debt, and your ability to succeed? Make it empowering. Make it true for you.

Find your accountability partner. Ask someone to play this role. Schedule your first check-in. Commit to regular meetings.

This assignment will take several hours spread over a few days. Do not rush it. Quality matters more than speed. These documents become the constitution of You, Inc. They guide everything that follows. Do this work well and everything else becomes easier.

Most people will not complete this assignment. They will

read this chapter and move to Chapter 2 without doing the work. Those people will fail at budgeting. Their budgets will lack purpose. Their sacrifices will feel meaningless. They will quit when budgeting gets hard.

You will complete this assignment. You will build your foundation correctly. You will have purpose, direction, targets, values, beliefs, and accountability. You will succeed where others fail because you did the work they refused to do.

CHAPTER 2
TRACK YOUR MONEY: THE ONE-MONTH AUDIT

Most people think their problem is not enough money. What they usually have is not enough truth.

They guess where their money goes. They estimate. They assume. They rely on memory. And then they wonder why their plans don't work. But money does not respond to intentions. It responds to behavior. And behavior can only be governed when it is visible.

That is why this chapter matters so much.

Before you attempt to increase income, before you allocate a single dollar, before you cut an expense or choose a tool, you must confront reality. Not your ideal month. Not your best month. Not the version of yourself you hope to be. You must look at what is actually happening.

This is the one-month audit. It is not punishment. It is leadership. Every well-run business knows exactly where its money goes. Your household deserves the same level of respect.

The Business Parallel: You Cannot Improve What You Do Not Measure

Every successful business runs internal audits. Monthly reviews. Quarterly assessments. Annual evaluations. These audits answer critical questions: Where is revenue coming from? Where are costs going? What processes waste money? What inefficiencies exist? What patterns emerge over time?

No business operates blind. No CEO says "I think we spent about $50,000 on office supplies last quarter, but I'm not sure." That CEO gets fired. Businesses track everything because tracking creates the visibility needed to make intelligent decisions.

Your household is a business. You, Inc. generates revenue through your labor. You, Inc. has operational costs. You, Inc. has waste points and inefficiencies. You, Inc. has spending patterns. But unlike a corporation with accountants and analysts, You, Inc. probably tracks nothing. You operate blind. You guess. You estimate. You hope.

This is why You, Inc. fails financially while generating decent revenue.

A business cannot improve operations until it measures operations. A factory cannot reduce waste until it identifies waste. A retail store cannot optimize inventory until it tracks inventory. Measurement comes first. Improvement comes second. This sequence never reverses.

The same principle applies to your money. You cannot improve your financial situation until you measure your financial situation. You cannot reduce waste until you identify waste. You cannot optimize spending until you track spending. The one-month audit is your measurement. Everything else builds on this foundation.

Corporations understand something most families do not: data creates clarity, clarity creates control, and control creates power. When a business reviews its profit and loss statement, that statement contains no opinions or emotions. Just numbers. Revenue minus expenses equals profit or loss. The statement reveals truth. The business uses that truth to make better decisions next month.

Your one-month audit does the same thing. It creates a profit and loss statement for You, Inc. Income minus expenses equals surplus or deficit. The audit reveals truth. You use that truth to make better decisions next month.

But here is what makes families different from corporations: corporations welcome audits because audits expose opportunities to increase profit. Families resist audits because audits expose behavior they feel ashamed about. A business sees waste as a problem to fix. A person sees waste as a moral failure.

This thinking is wrong. Waste is not a moral failure. Waste is a management problem. You were never taught to manage money. You were never taught to track spending. You were never taught to audit your finances. Your waste exists because you lack systems, not because you lack character.

The audit removes emotion from the equation. The audit says "Here is what happened last month. Here are the numbers. No judgment. Just data." You use that data to build better systems. This is business thinking applied to personal finance.

Why do corporations run monthly reviews instead of annual reviews? Because monthly data catches problems early. A business that reviews finances once per year discovers problems too late to fix them easily. A business that reviews monthly spots trends, adjusts quickly, and prevents small issues from becoming catastrophic.

You, Inc. needs the same frequency. You will track monthly. You will review weekly. You will catch problems early. You will adjust quickly. This is how businesses stay profitable. This is how you build wealth.

Tracking is not punishment. Tracking is data collection.

Data is power. Data reveals what works and what fails. Data shows you exactly where your money creates value and where it disappears into nothing. Without data, you are guessing. With data, you are managing.

Most people resist tracking because they do not want to face the truth. They prefer comfortable ignorance over uncomfortable knowledge. But comfortable ignorance keeps you broke. Uncomfortable knowledge builds wealth. Choose knowledge.

The Theological Anchor: God Works Through Order, Not Confusion

Scripture speaks directly to the practice of financial tracking, though it uses the language of farming and shepherding instead of accounting. Proverbs 27:23-24 says: "Know well the condition of your flocks, and give attention to your herds, for riches do not last forever; and does a crown endure to all generations?"

The shepherd had to track his animals. He counted them. He knew which ones were healthy and which were sick. He knew which pastures produced the best grazing. He knew when to move the flock and when to stay. This knowledge came from constant attention and observation. The shepherd who did not track his flock lost animals to wolves, disease, and theft. The shepherd who tracked his flock protected his livelihood.

This is financial tracking in ancient terms. Your money is your flock. Your expenses are the pastures where your money grazes. You must know the condition of your money. You must give attention to where it goes. You must count it. You must observe patterns. You must protect it from waste, from impulse, from theft through fees and interest.

The shepherd who ignores his flock loses everything. The person who ignores their money loses everything. This is not complicated theology. This is practical wisdom recorded three thousand years ago and still true today.

First Corinthians 14:40 says: "But all things should be done decently and in order." Order requires knowledge. You cannot create order in your finances without knowing what currently exists. Chaos comes from ignorance. Order comes from visibility. God works through order, not confusion.

When your money is disordered, your life is disordered. When you do not know where your money goes, you cannot know if you are managing it well. When you cannot manage it well, you cannot multiply it. When you cannot multiply it, you fail the most basic test of stewardship.

Consider the parable of the talents in Matthew 25:14-30. The master entrusted different amounts to three servants. The master knew exactly what he gave to each one. He tracked it. He expected an accounting. When he returned, he demanded to know what happened with his resources. The servants who multiplied their talents were rewarded. The servant who buried his talent out of fear was rebuked.

The master could only hold the servants accountable because the master tracked what he gave them. Without tracking, there is no accountability. Without accountability, there is no growth. Without growth, resources stagnate and waste.

You are both master and servant in your financial life. God is the ultimate master who entrusted resources to you. You are the steward who must multiply those resources. But you also serve as master over your household. You must track what you have. You must demand accountability from yourself. You must know whether you are multiplying resources or burying them.

Tracking creates the visibility that makes accountability possible. Without tracking, you can deceive yourself indefinitely. You can tell yourself you are doing fine while you are actually failing. You can believe you are managing well while you are wasting resources. Tracking ends the self-deception. Tracking reveals truth.

Many people feel shame around money. They do not want to track because they fear what they will discover. They do not want to see their failures documented. They do not want to confront their waste. This shame keeps them trapped in ignorance and poverty.

But shame is not from God. Conviction is from God. Conviction says "You are capable of better. Here is the truth. Now make changes." Shame says "You are worthless. You always fail. Do not even try." Conviction leads to growth. Shame leads to paralysis.

The audit is conviction, not shame. The audit says "Here is what happened. Here is the truth. You are capable of better. Now make changes." Accept the conviction. Reject the shame. Use the truth to build something better.

God gave you resources for a reason. Those resources are not punishment. Those resources are not irrelevant. Those resources are assignments. You have rent or a mortgage because you need shelter to fulfill your purpose. You have food expenses because you need strength to work. You have transportation costs because you need mobility to serve. Every category of spending exists to support your mission.

But when spending exceeds what serves your mission, waste occurs. When you spend money on things that do not advance your purpose, you are misallocating God's resources. This is not efficient stewardship. This is not multiplying your talent. This is burying your talent in entertainment, impulse purchases, and lifestyle inflation.

The audit reveals where you serve your mission and where you waste your assignment. This revelation is not condemnation. This revelation is grace. God loves you enough to show you the truth so you can fix it. Accept the grace. Do the audit. See the truth. Make changes.

Why People Avoid Tracking – And Why This Avoidance Keeps Them Poor

Here is what happens when you do not track:

You spend $5 here and $10 there and $20 somewhere else. None of those transactions feel significant. $5 is nothing. $10 is nothing. $20 is nothing. So you keep spending small amounts without thinking about it.

Then the month ends. Your bank account is empty. You have no idea where the money went. You tell yourself you will do better next month. Next month comes. Same result.

This cycle continues for years. Decades. Your entire life.

The audit breaks the cycle. The audit forces you to see. Once you see, you cannot unsee. Once you know, you cannot unknown.

That is why most people resist the audit. They know the audit will reveal uncomfortable truths. They know they will have to change. Change is hard. Ignorance is easy.

But ignorance is also expensive. Ignorance is why you have no savings. Ignorance is why you are in debt. Ignorance is why you are reading this book.

Let me tell you exactly why people avoid tracking and why this avoidance guarantees poverty.

Fear of judgment. People fear what they will discover about themselves. They fear seeing proof of their failures. They fear confirming what they suspect: they waste money, they lack discipline, they make bad decisions. So they avoid tracking to avoid confronting these truths. But avoiding the truth does not change the truth. The waste continues whether you track it or not. The difference is that tracked waste can be fixed. Untracked waste cannot.

Overwhelm. People think tracking is complicated and time-consuming. They imagine spreadsheets with hundreds of rows and complex formulas. They imagine spending hours every week managing numbers. This assumption is wrong.

Tracking takes five minutes per day with modern tools. But the assumption creates enough resistance that they never start. They choose ignorance over five minutes of daily effort.

Pride. People do not want to admit they need help. They do not want to admit they lack financial discipline. They do not want to admit they are bad with money. Tracking feels like admitting failure. So they avoid tracking to preserve their self-image. But the self-image is false. They are already bad with money. Avoiding tracking just prevents improvement.

Immediate discomfort vs. delayed benefit. Tracking creates immediate discomfort. You see waste. You see impulse purchases. You see money disappearing into categories you cannot justify. This discomfort is unpleasant. The benefits of tracking are delayed. Better financial decisions happen over weeks and months, not days. Most people choose immediate comfort over delayed benefits. This choice keeps them poor.

Lack of consequences. Not tracking has no immediate consequences. You do not get fired from your life for failing to track spending. No authority figure demands monthly reports. You face no penalties for ignorance. So people drift without tracking for decades because nothing forces them to start. But the long-term consequence is poverty. The consequence is working until you die. The consequence is never retiring. The consequence is stress and debt and financial failure. These consequences are real. These consequences are severe. These consequences are guaranteed. But they arrive slowly, so people ignore them.

All these reasons are excuses. All these excuses keep you broke. Tracking is not complicated. Tracking is not time-consuming. Tracking is not shameful. Tracking is necessary. Tracking is how you gain visibility over your financial life. Tracking is how you identify waste. Tracking is how you make better decisions. Tracking is how you build wealth.

You will track because you are serious about change. You will track because you refuse to stay ignorant. You will track because you want wealth more than you want comfort. You will track because tracking is the foundation of all financial success.

Why One Month?

You need 30 days minimum to capture a complete picture of your spending.

One week is not enough. Your spending changes throughout the month. You might have expenses at the beginning of the month that do not repeat later. You might have expenses at the end of the month that do not show up at the beginning.

One month captures everything. Recurring bills. Variable expenses. Impulse purchases. Forgotten subscriptions. Emergency expenses. Social spending. Everything.

Some people want to track for two or three months to get an even better picture. Fine. Do that if you want. But do not use "I need more data" as an excuse to delay action. One month is enough to start making changes.

Start the audit on the first day of the month. Track every dollar until the last day of the month. Then analyze. Then adjust. Then implement your budget the following month.

Do not start mid-month. Do not skip days. Do not estimate days you forgot to track. Track every single day for 30 consecutive days.

Pick Your Tracking Method

You have three options for tracking your spending. Each method works. Each method has strengths and weaknesses. Pick the one that matches your habits and stick with it for the full 30 days.

Option 1: Pen and Paper

Get a small notebook. Something you can carry in your pocket or purse. Keep it with you everywhere. Every time you spend money, write it down immediately.

Write the date. Write what you bought. Write how much you spent. Write the category (food, gas, entertainment, etc.).

Do this the moment you spend. Do not wait until you get home. Do not wait until the end of the day. Immediate tracking is accurate tracking. Delayed tracking is guessing.

Strengths of this method:

No technology required. No apps to download. No accounts to set up. Just a notebook and a pen.

No distractions. You are not opening your phone and getting sucked into social media while trying to track expenses.

Forces you to be conscious of every purchase. When you have to physically write down every expense, you become more aware of your spending. That awareness alone often reduces spending.

Weaknesses of this method:

Easy to forget. You forget the notebook at home. You forget to write something down. You lose the notebook.

Requires discipline. You must remember to carry the notebook everywhere. You must remember to write down every transaction. Most people do not have that discipline.

Manual calculation. At the end of the month, you have to add up all the numbers yourself. This takes time and introduces the possibility of math errors.

Who this method works for:

People who do not use technology much. People who prefer

analog systems. People who have strong habits and routines. People who are disciplined enough to carry the notebook everywhere and write down every transaction without fail.

If you choose this method, buy two notebooks. Keep one in your car and one in your bag. That way if you forget one, you have a backup.

Option 2: Spreadsheet

Create a simple spreadsheet. You can use Excel, Google Sheets, or any spreadsheet program.

Set up columns for: Date, Category, Description, Amount.

Every day, open the spreadsheet and enter your transactions. Do this at the same time every day. Morning with your coffee. Evening before bed. Lunch break at work. Pick a time and make it a habit.

Strengths of this method:

Automatic calculations. The spreadsheet adds up your totals automatically. No math errors.

Easy to categorize. You can sort and filter by category to see where your money is going.

Customizable. You can add columns, create formulas, build charts, track trends over time.

No recurring costs. Once you create the spreadsheet, you own it forever. No subscriptions. No fees.

Weaknesses of this method:

Requires daily discipline. You must remember to update the spreadsheet every single day. If you wait until the end of the week, you will forget transactions.

Not portable. You need a computer or tablet to update the

spreadsheet. If you are out and about, you cannot track in real time.

Manual entry. You still have to type in every transaction. This takes time.

Who this method works for:

People who work at computers all day. People who like customization and control. People who already use spreadsheets for other things. People who are disciplined enough to update the spreadsheet daily without skipping.

If you choose this method, keep a small notebook with you during the day to jot down expenses. Then transfer those expenses to the spreadsheet every evening. Do not skip the evening update. If you skip one day, you will skip two days. If you skip two days, you will quit.

Option 3: Budget App

Download a budget app on your phone. Connect your bank accounts and credit cards to the app. The app automatically imports every transaction. You just review the transactions and make sure they are categorized correctly.

Popular apps include:

- Mint (free).
- PocketGuard (free and paid versions).
- YNAB - You Need A Budget (paid subscription).
- EveryDollar (free and paid versions).
- Good budget (free and paid versions).

I recommend Mint for most people. It is free. It is easy to use. It connects to almost every bank and credit card. It categorizes most transactions automatically.

Strengths of this method:

Automatic tracking. Once you set it up, the app tracks everything for you. No manual entry. No forgetting to write things down.

Real-time updates. Every transaction shows up in the app within a day or two. You can see your spending in real time.

Visual reports. Most apps show you charts and graphs of your spending. You can see exactly where your money goes.

Alerts and reminders. Apps can send you notifications when you overspend in a category or when bills are due.

Weaknesses of this method:

Requires technology. You need a smartphone. You need to download the app. You need to connect your accounts. Some people are not comfortable with this.

Privacy concerns. You are giving the app access to your financial accounts. The good apps use bank-level security, but some people do not trust it.

Imperfect categorization. Apps sometimes categorize transactions wrong. A purchase at Target might get categorized as groceries when it was actually clothes. You have to review and fix these.

Cash transactions. If you use cash, the app does not see it. You have to manually enter cash transactions.

Who this method works for:

Most people. This is the easiest method. This is the method that requires the least discipline. This is the method I recommend unless you have a strong reason to use one of the other methods.

If you choose this method, download the app today. Set it up today. Connect your accounts today. Do not wait. Do not delay. The sooner you start tracking, the sooner you see the truth.

Which Method Should You Choose?

Ask yourself these questions:

- Do you carry your phone everywhere? Use an app.
- Do you hate technology? Use pen and paper.
- Do you work at a computer all day? Use a spreadsheet.
- Do you forget to track things? Use an app (it tracks automatically).
- Do you use cash for most purchases? Use pen and paper or spreadsheet (apps do not track cash well).
- Do you want detailed customization? Use a spreadsheet.
- Do you want simple and automatic? Use an app.

Pick one method. Commit to it for 30 days. Do not switch methods mid-month. Do not use multiple methods. One method. 30 days. Full commitment.

Track Everything

When I say track everything, I mean everything.

- The $2 coffee. The $1 gum.
- The $5 parking fee. T
- he $3 ATM fee.
- The $10 app subscription.
- The $15 you gave your kid for lunch.
- The $20 you spent at the gas station.
- The $8 you spent at the vending machine. Everything.

Small expenses destroy budgets.

You think $3 per day does not matter. Let me show you why you are wrong:

$3 per day = $21 per week = $90 per month = $1,080 per year.

That is $1,080 you could save. That is $1,080 toward your emergency fund. That is $1,080 toward your down payment. That is $1,080 toward getting out of debt.

Multiply that by all your small daily expenses. Coffee. Snacks. Fast food. Parking. ATM fees. Vending machines. Convenience store runs.

Most people waste $200-$500 per month on small expenses they do not even notice. That is $2,400 to $6,000 per year. That is life-changing money you are throwing away.

Here is what people tell me when I say to track everything:

"But $2 for coffee does not matter." Yes it does. Track it.

"But I cannot write down every little thing." Yes you can. Track it.

"But it takes too much time." It takes 10 seconds. Track it.

"But I will forget." Then you are not serious about changing. Track it.

People resist tracking small expenses because they do not want to admit how much they waste. They do not want to see the truth. They want to keep their comfortable ignorance.

You are not those people. You are serious about change. Track everything.

Cash Transactions

If you use cash, you must track it manually. Apps cannot see cash transactions.

Every time you withdraw cash from an ATM, write down how much you withdrew. Then write down every purchase you make with that cash.

If you cannot track your cash spending, stop using cash. Use your debit card for everything during the audit month. That way your transactions show up automatically in your bank account and your budget app.

Shared Expenses

If you share expenses with a spouse or partner, you need to track their spending too.

Some apps allow multiple users on the same account. Set that up. Make sure both of you are tracking.

If your spouse refuses to track, you have a bigger problem than budgeting. You have a partnership problem. You cannot build wealth if one person is tracking and one person is sabotaging. Have that conversation now.

Kids and Dependents

If you give money to your kids, track it. If you pay for their activities, track it. If you buy their clothes, track it.

Many parents underestimate how much they spend on their kids. They think it is just school supplies and clothes. Then they track it and realize they are spending $300-$500 per month on sports, activities, entertainment, eating out, and impulse purchases.

Track all of it. You need to see the full picture.

Categorize Your Expenses

As you track, categorize each expense. Most budget apps do this automatically. If you are using pen and paper or a spreadsheet, write the category next to each expense.

Here are the 14 categories I recommend:

1. Housing:

Rent or mortgage, property taxes, homeowners insurance, renters insurance, HOA fees, home maintenance, repairs, lawn care, cleaning service, pest control.

This is usually your biggest expense category. For most people, housing should be 25-30% of take-home income. If your housing is more than 35% of income, you have a problem. We will address that in Chapter 5.

2. Transportation

Car payment, car insurance, gas, oil changes, maintenance, repairs, car washes, registration, parking, tolls, rideshare (Uber, Lyft), public transportation, taxis.

Transportation is usually the second biggest expense category. For most people, transportation should be 15-20% of take-home income. If your transportation is more than 25%, you are spending too much on your car.

3. Utilities

Electric, gas, water, sewer, trash, internet, phone (cell and landline if you still have one), streaming services (Netflix, Hulu, Disney+, etc.).

Wait. Streaming services are not utilities. I know. But most people pay for them monthly like utilities, so I put them here. If you want to categorize streaming as entertainment, fine. Pick one category and be consistent.

Utilities should be 5-10% of income. If your utilities are higher than that, you need to find ways to reduce usage or switch providers.

4. Food

Groceries, restaurants, fast food, coffee shops, food delivery (DoorDash, Uber Eats, etc.), vending machines, convenience store snacks, work lunches, alcohol.

Food is where most people lose control. Groceries are planned. Restaurants are impulse. Coffee shops are habit. Delivery is convenience. All of it adds up fast.

Separate groceries from eating out when you categorize. You need to see how much you spend on each. Groceries should be 10-15% of income. Eating out should be 0-5% of income. If you are spending more than 20% of income on food total, you are eating your savings.

5. Personal Care

Haircuts, hair coloring, barber, salon, nails, makeup, skincare, toiletries, gym membership, fitness classes, massages, spa treatments.

Personal care should be 2-5% of income. Many women spend 10-15% on personal care. Many men spend less than 2%. Track what you actually spend, then decide if it is worth it.

6. Clothing

Clothes, shoes, accessories, jewelry, alterations, dry cleaning, laundry service.

Clothing should be 2-5% of income. Many people spend 10-15% because they buy things they do not need. We will address this in Chapter 5.

7. Health

Health insurance premiums, dental insurance, vision insurance, copays, prescriptions, over-the-counter medications, supplements, medical equipment, therapy, counseling.

Health expenses are necessary. Do not cut these. But do shop around for insurance. Do use generic medications. Do ask for payment plans. Health should be 5-10% of income if you have insurance. If you do not have insurance, get insurance. You are one medical emergency away from bankruptcy.

8. Entertainment

Cable TV, streaming services (if you did not categorize under utilities), movies, concerts, sporting events, hobbies, books, magazines, subscriptions (if not already categorized), video games, music, apps.

Entertainment is a luxury. Entertainment should be 2-5% of income. If you are broke and in debt, entertainment should be 0% of income. We will address this in Chapter 5.

9. Debt Payments

Credit card payments, student loans, personal loans, medical debt, car loans (if not categorized under transportation), payday loans, any other debt.

Track the total payment, not just the interest. If you pay $300 toward your credit card, track $300. Do not separate principal and interest. You need to know how much cash is leaving your account each month for debt.

Debt payments should be as low as possible. If your debt payments are more than 20% of income, you have a debt crisis. You need to get aggressive about paying off debt.

10. Savings and Investments

Emergency fund contributions, retirement contributions (401k, IRA, etc.), brokerage account deposits, college savings (529 plans), any other savings or investments.

Savings should be at least 20% of income. If you are not saving 20%, you are not building wealth. If you are not saving anything, you are broke even if you make good money.

Most people track savings as what is left over after expenses. Wrong. Savings is an expense. Savings is the first expense you pay. Pay yourself first. We will talk more about this in Chapter 3.

11. Childcare and Education

Daycare, preschool, after-school care, babysitters, nannies, school tuition, school supplies, school fees, tutoring, kids' activities (sports, music, dance, etc.), kids' allowances.

If you have kids, this category can be huge. Track it all. You need to see how much your kids actually cost. Then you can make informed decisions about which activities are worth it and which ones need to go.

12. Pets

Pet food, veterinarian visits, medications, grooming, boarding, pet insurance, toys, treats.

Pets cost more than people think. The average dog costs $1,000-$2,000 per year. The average cat costs $500-$1,000 per year. Track your pet expenses so you know the real cost.

13. Gifts and Donations

Birthday gifts, holiday gifts, wedding gifts, baby shower gifts, charitable donations, church offerings, fundraisers, GoFundMe contributions, tips (if you tip regularly).

Gifts and donations should be 2-5% of income. Many people spend 10-15% during holidays. Plan for this. Set aside money each month so holiday spending does not destroy your budget.

14. Other

Anything that does not fit the categories above. Legal fees. Accounting fees. Bank fees. ATM fees. Late fees. Overdraft fees. Postage. Fees for anything.

If you have a lot of expenses in the Other category, create new categories. The goal is to categorize everything so you can see patterns.

Review and Fix Categories

Most budget apps categorize automatically. The apps are usually right. Sometimes they are wrong.

A purchase at Target might get categorized as groceries when you actually bought clothes.

A purchase at a gas station might get categorized as gas when you actually bought snacks.

A purchase at Walmart might get categorized as groceries when you bought electronics.

Review every transaction. Fix wrong categories. Accuracy matters.

If you are not sure which category to use, pick one and be consistent. The goal is not perfect categories. The goal is to see patterns in your spending.

The Awakening Moment

At the end of 30 days, total each category.

Look at the numbers.

This is the awakening moment.

This is the moment when you see the truth about your spending. This is the moment when excuses stop working. This is the moment when you either commit to change or go back to being broke.

Most people see these totals and feel sick.

> They spent $400 eating out when they thought they spent $150.
> They spent $200 on coffee when they thought they spent $50.
> They spent $150 on subscriptions they do not use.
> They spent $300 on clothes they do not need.
> They spent $100 on impulse purchases they do not remember.
> They spent $80 on ATM fees and bank fees because they cannot manage their account.
> They wasted $1,200 that month. $14,400 per year.
> Money that could have been saved. Money that could have eliminated debt. Money that could have bought a home.

Do not skip this step. Do not estimate. Do not guess. Add up the actual numbers from your actual spending.

Write the total for each category on a piece of paper. Make the numbers big. Make them visible.

Put that paper somewhere you will see it every day. The refrigerator. Your bathroom mirror. Your car dashboard. Your wallet.

You need to see these numbers. You need to feel the weight of them. You need to understand that your current spending is why you have no savings. Your current spending is why you are in debt. Your current spending is why you cannot buy a home.

This is not about shame. This is not about beating yourself up. This is about clarity.

You cannot fix what you cannot see. Now you see.

Calculate Spending as Percentage of Income

Now take each category total and calculate it as a percentage of your take-home income.

Here is the formula: (Category Total ÷ Monthly Take-Home Income) × 100 = Percentage

Example: You spent $800 on food. Your monthly take-home income is $4,000. ($800 ÷ $4,000) × 100 = 20%

You spent 20% of your income on food.

Do this for every category. Write the percentage next to the dollar amount.

Now compare your percentages to the recommended percentages:

- Housing: 25-30%
- Transportation: 15-20%
- Utilities: 5-10%
- Food: 10-15%
- Savings: 20%
- Everything else: 10-20%

If your percentages are higher than recommended, you have a problem. We will fix this in Chapter 5.

If your savings percentage is zero, you have a crisis. We will fix this in Chapter 3.

Classify Your Expenses: High, Average, Low Priority

Now take each category and classify it as high, average, or low priority.

This is where most people lie to themselves. They want everything to be high priority. They want to believe they need everything they are spending money on.

You do not need everything. You want everything. There is a difference.

Here is how to classify:

High Priority Expenses

These are mandatory expenses you cannot eliminate without creating a crisis.

- Rent or mortgage.
- Utilities (electric, gas, water, trash).
- Minimum debt payments.
- Health insurance.
- Car insurance (if you must drive for work).
- Groceries (not restaurants, groceries).
- Essential medications.
- Childcare (if you must work).

That is it. That is the high priority list.
Notice what is not on the list:

- Cable TV.
- Streaming services.
- Gym membership.
- Eating out.
- Coffee shops.
- New clothes.

- Entertainment.
- Hobbies.
- Vacations.

Those are not high priority. Those are luxuries.

High priority expenses are non-negotiable. You pay these first. If you cannot afford these, you have a crisis and you need to make major changes immediately (move to cheaper housing, sell your car, find cheaper insurance, etc.).

Average Priority Expenses

These are expenses you need but you have some flexibility. You cannot eliminate them completely but you can reduce them.

- Gas (you could drive less or take public transportation).
- Phone (you need a phone but maybe not unlimited data).
- Internet (you need it for work but maybe not the fastest plan).
- Clothing (you need clothes but not new clothes every month).
- Personal care (you need haircuts but maybe not every three weeks).
- Pet care (you committed to the pet so you must care for it, but you can reduce costs).

Average priority expenses are negotiable. You keep them but you look for ways to reduce them.

Low Priority Expenses

These are expenses you do not need. These are wants, not needs.

- Restaurants and eating out.
- Coffee shops.
- Alcohol.
- Streaming services.
- Cable TV.
- Gym memberships (you can exercise for free).
- Entertainment (movies, concerts, etc.).
- Hobbies.
- Subscriptions (magazines, apps, services).
- New clothes (beyond basics).
- Jewelry and accessories.
- Vacations.
- Gifts beyond immediate family.

Low priority expenses are the first things you cut. These are luxuries. Luxuries are for people who have savings and no debt.

If you have no savings and you have debt, you have no business spending money on luxuries. Period. No exceptions. No justifications.

Here is what people say when I tell them this:

"But I need my gym membership to stay healthy." No you do not. You can run outside. You can do pushups at home. You can watch free workout videos on YouTube. The gym is a luxury.

"But I need my streaming services to relax." No you do not. You can read a book from the library. You can watch free content on YouTube. You can spend time with family. Streaming is a luxury.

"But I need to eat out because I am too busy to cook." No you are not. You watch TV three hours per night. You scroll social media two hours per day. You have time. You choose not to use it for cooking. Eating out is a luxury.

"But I deserve to enjoy my life." You do deserve to enjoy your life. You do not deserve to be broke. You do not deserve to be in debt. You do not deserve to be stressed about money. Cut the luxuries now so you can afford luxuries later.

Go through your expense list right now. Mark each category H (high), A (average), or L (low).

Be honest. Most people lie to themselves here. They classify wants as needs because they do not want to give up their comfortable lifestyle.

Your comfortable lifestyle is why you are broke. Give it up now so you can have a better lifestyle later.

Calculate Your Spending by Priority

Now add up your spending in each priority level:

Total High Priority Expenses: $_____ Total Average Priority Expenses: $_____ Total Low Priority Expenses: $_____

Look at your low priority total.

That number represents money you are wasting every month. That number represents money you could save. That number represents money that could be building wealth. That number represents money that could be buying your freedom from debt. That number represents money that could be buying your home.

For most people, low priority expenses are $300-$800 per month. Some people waste $1,000-$2,000 per month on low priority expenses.

That is $3,600 to $24,000 per year. Life-changing money. Down payment money. Debt elimination money. Emergency fund money. Retirement money.

You are throwing it away on restaurants and coffee and subscriptions and entertainment.

If your low priority expenses are more than $100 per month, you have work to do. We will address this in Chapter 5.

If your low priority expenses are more than your savings, you have a crisis. You are prioritizing fun over your future. That stops now.

Compare Spending to Income

Take your total monthly expenses (all categories combined). Write that number down.

Now write down your monthly take-home income. This is your income after taxes, after insurance, after retirement contributions. This is the money that actually hits your bank account.

Do not use your gross income. Do not use your salary. Use your actual take-home pay.

Subtract expenses from income:
Monthly Take-Home Income: $_____ Total Monthly Expenses: $_____ Difference: $_____

Now look at that difference. This number tells you everything you need to know about your financial situation.

If the Difference is Positive

You have money left over. Good.

But here is the question: Where did that money go?

If you did not save it, you wasted it. You spent it on something you did not track. You withdrew cash and do not remember what you bought. You made impulse purchases. You lost it.

Most people who have money left over do not save it. They waste it. They let it sit in their checking account until they spend it on something they do not need.

This is why people who make good money are still broke. They make enough to save but they do not save. They spend everything they make.

If you have a positive difference but no savings, you are wasting that difference. That stops now. In Chapter 3, we will set up automatic savings so this cannot happen.

If the Difference is Negative

You are spending more than you make. You are going into debt every month. You are one emergency away from disaster. This is a crisis.

How are you covering the difference? Credit cards? Payday loans? Borrowing from family? Not paying bills?

Whatever you are doing, it is not sustainable. You cannot spend more than you make forever. Eventually you will hit the limit. Eventually the debt will crush you. Eventually you will lose everything.

You must make major changes immediately. Not next month. Not after the holidays. Not when things calm down. Now.

You have three options:

1. Increase income dramatically (get a second job, work overtime, start a side business).
2. Cut expenses dramatically (move to cheaper housing, sell your car, eliminate all non-essential spending).
3. Do both (increase income and cut expenses at the same time).

I recommend option 3. We will cover income strategies in Chapter 4 and expense cutting in Chapter 5.

But understand this: If you are spending more than you make, you do not have a budget problem. You have a lifestyle problem. Your lifestyle costs more than you can afford. Change your lifestyle or stay broke forever.

If the Difference is Zero or Close to Zero

You are living paycheck to paycheck. You make just enough to cover your expenses. You have no margin for error. One unexpected expense destroys you.

You cannot afford to get sick. You cannot afford for your car to break down. You cannot afford for your rent to increase. You cannot afford for anything to go wrong.

This is not sustainable. This is stressful. This is dangerous.

You must create margin. You need at least $500 per month left over after expenses. That $500 goes to savings and debt elimination.

How do you create margin? Increase income or cut expenses or both. Same as above. Chapters 4 and 5 will show you how.

But understand this: If you have zero margin, you are broke even if you are not in debt. You are one emergency away from going into debt. You are one lost job away from losing everything.

Create margin. Build savings. Get ahead of your expenses. This is not optional.

The Hard Truth About Your Spending

Here is what most people discover during the one-month audit:

They spend more than they think.

You thought you spent $100 on coffee. You spent $200. You thought you spent $300 eating out. You spent $600. You thought you spent $50 on subscriptions. You spent $150.

Every category is higher than you estimated. Why? Because you do not track. Because you make purchases and forget them. Because you underestimate how much small purchases add up.

The audit does not lie. The audit shows you the truth.

They waste more than they realize.

You wasted money on subscriptions you do not use. You wasted money on food that went bad. You wasted money on fees because you cannot manage your account. You wasted money on impulse purchases you regret.

Add up all the waste. For most people, waste is $200-$500 per month. That is $2,400-$6,000 per year. That is a down payment on a house. That is an emergency fund. That is freedom from debt.

You threw it away.

They have less control than they believed.

You thought you were managing your money. You were not. Your money was managing you.

You thought you were making conscious decisions. You were not. You were reacting. You were spending without thinking. You were letting your emotions and impulses control your money.

The audit reveals lack of control. Once you see it, you can fix it. But first you have to see it.

They have been lying to themselves.

You told yourself you do not make enough money to save. The audit showed you waste $400 per month. You make enough. You just spend it on things you do not need.

You told yourself you do not have a spending problem. The audit showed you spent 30% of your income eating out. You have a spending problem.

You told yourself you are doing fine. The audit showed you are spending more than you make. You are not doing fine. You are going broke slowly.

The audit ends the lies. The audit forces you to face reality.

Accept the Truth and Commit to Change

This is uncomfortable. This is supposed to be uncomfortable. Comfort is what got you here. Discomfort is what gets you out.

Do not ignore what the audit reveals. Do not make excuses. Do not justify unnecessary spending.

"I work hard so I deserve to treat myself." You do not deserve to be broke. Cut the spending.

"I will start saving when I make more money." You will not. You will spend more when you make more. Cut the spending now.

"My life is stressful and spending money makes me feel better." Your life is stressful because you have no money. Spending more money makes you more stressed. Cut the spending.

"I do not spend that much compared to other people." I do not care what other people spend. Other people are broke too. Cut the spending.

Stop making excuses. Look at the numbers. Accept the truth. Commit to change.

The one-month audit shows you where you are. The rest of this book shows you how to get where you want to go.

But you must start with truth. You must see your actual spending. You must face the reality of your financial situation.

Most People Will Not Do This

Most people will not do this audit. They will skip this chapter. They will tell themselves they already know their spending. They will create a budget based on guesses. Then their budget will fail within two weeks.

Then they will say budgeting does not work. Budgeting works. They just did not work the budget.

You are not most people.

You are going to do the audit. You are going to track every dollar for 30 days. You are going to categorize every expense. You are going to classify every expense. You are going to calculate your totals. You are going to compare spending to income.

You are going to see the truth. Then you are going to accept the truth. Then you are going to change.

The Bridge to Revenue: What Tracking Reveals About Income

You now have complete visibility over your spending. You know where every dollar goes. You have categorized your expenses. You have calculated your priorities. You have compared spending to income. You have seen the truth.

But here is what the audit also revealed: spending is only half the equation.

You tracked expenses. You identified waste. You saw where money disappears. This is critical information. But now you must ask the question that separates people who budget from people who build wealth:

Is the problem only how much you spend, or is the problem also how much you earn?

For some people, the audit reveals massive waste. They spend $500 per month on low priority expenses. They eat out constantly. They buy things they do not need. Their problem is spending. Cut the waste. Save the money. Build wealth.

For other people, the audit reveals something different. They spend responsibly. They do not waste money on luxuries. They cook at home. They drive used cars. They live modestly. But their income is too low. They barely cover essentials. They have nothing left to save. Their problem is not spending. Their problem is income.

For most people, the problem is both. They waste some money on unnecessary expenses. But even if they eliminated all waste, their income would still be barely enough to survive, let alone build wealth.

This is where the business parallel becomes critical. A business cannot survive on cost-cutting alone. A business that reduces expenses but generates no revenue goes bankrupt slowly instead of quickly. The result is the same. Bankruptcy.

You, Inc. cannot build wealth on expense reduction alone. You must generate revenue. You must increase income. You must treat income as a strategic priority, not as a fixed constraint.

Without financial truth, income strategy is aimless. You cannot know how much extra income you need until you know your current spending and your future goals. The audit gives you this baseline. Now you can calculate exactly how much additional income would transform your situation.

Without income strategy, financial truth is powerless. You can track every dollar perfectly. You can cut every unnecessary expense. But if your income is insufficient, tracking and cutting will never build wealth. They will only slow the descent into poverty.

The next step is revenue. The next step is increasing your earning capacity. The next step is treating income as a design project instead of accepting it as fate.

You did the hard work of facing truth about spending. Now you will do the hard work of building strategy around income. You will learn how businesses think about revenue generation. You will apply those principles to your household. You will increase your income intentionally, strategically, and systematically.

This is where wealth building accelerates. This is where good budgeting becomes great wealth. This is where You, Inc. transforms from managing scarcity to creating abundance.

The audit ended with truth about spending. The income chapter begins with strategy about earning. Together, they create the complete financial picture that builds lasting wealth.

Your Assignment for This Chapter

Do not move to Chapter 3 until you complete this assignment.

- **Step 1:** Pick your tracking method (app, spreadsheet, or pen and paper). Set it up today.
- **Step 2:** Track every dollar you spend for the next 30 days. No exceptions. No skipping days. No estimating.
- **Step 3:** At the end of 30 days, total each category.
- **Step 4:** Calculate each category as a percentage of income.
- **Step 5:** Classify each category as high, average, or low priority.
- **Step 6:** Calculate total spending by priority level.
- **Step 7:** Compare total spending to income. Calculate the difference.
- **Step 8:** Write all these numbers on a piece of paper. Post it where you will see it every day.
- **Step 9:** Stare at those numbers. Feel the discomfort. Accept the truth.
- **Step 10:** Commit to change.

Then come back to Chapter 3.

The audit is the foundation. Without the audit, everything else fails.

Do the work!

At the end of the month, sit with the data. Don't defend it. Don't explain it away. Study it. Ask yourself simple, honest questions: Where is my money going? What does this say about my priorities? What patterns are helping me—and which ones are quietly holding me back?

This is not about judgment. It is about leadership.

Once you see the truth, something important happens: excuses lose their power. You can no longer blame confusion. You can no longer guess. You are now prepared to act intelligently.

And that brings us to the next chapter.

When people see their audit, they often realize the issue is not spending alone—it is income. The goals they want cannot be supported by what they earn. That is not failure. That is information.

Chapter 3 addresses that reality head-on. It is time to talk about revenue, earning power, and how You, Inc. must generate income that matches the future you are trying to build.

CHAPTER 3
REVENUE BEFORE BUDGETING

You can't allocate what you don't earn. A business can survive sloppy operations for a season, but it cannot survive without revenue. A household is no different.

This is where many financial books get the order wrong. They rush you into budgeting categories, expense trimming, and "money hacks" without asking the first and most basic question: Do you make enough to fund the life you are trying to build?

Income sets the boundary of your goals. If you want a $1 million home, but your income is $25,000 a year, the gap is not discipline alone—it is revenue. That doesn't mean the goal is impossible. It means the goal requires a different strategy: skill development, career movement, business creation, or multiple streams of income. It requires an income blueprint.

And there's also a spiritual truth here: your ability to produce is not an accident. Your gifts, your mind, your energy, your talent, your creativity—these are not random. They are entrusted.[3] You are responsible for how you develop them, how you deploy them, and what you do with what they produce.

So this chapter is not a motivational speech. It is an operational plan. It is You, Inc. building a top-line strategy—how you generate income, stabilize it, multiply it, and expand it over time.

Because nothing else in this book works at full power until revenue is addressed.

The Theology of Income: Why God Cares About Your Productivity

Your income is not just economic. It is spiritual. God does not give gifts for storage. He gives gifts for activation, expression, service, and multiplication.

Jesus taught this principle directly in the parable of the talents. Three servants received different sums. Two took action, traded, risked, produced, and multiplied. One buried his gift. The master praised the productive servants, saying: "Well done, good and faithful servant. You have been faithful over a little; I will set you over much."

But to the servant who buried his talent, the master declared: "You wicked and slothful servant."

The issue was not the amount each received. The issue was what they did with it.

This is a financial principle. It is a spiritual principle. It is a life principle. Income is not random. It is the harvest of your stewardship.

Scripture reinforces this repeatedly. Work produces profit: "In all toil there is profit, but mere talk tends only to poverty." Skill increases opportunity: "Do you see a man skillful in his work? He will stand before kings." Diligence leads to wealth: "The hand of the diligent makes rich." Wisdom attracts resources: "Wisdom gives life. Money is a protection."

Your income is the marketplace expression of your gifts,

diligence, wisdom, and stewardship. You are not called to bury your talent. You are called to multiply it.

Most people think about income passively. They wait for raises. They hope for bonuses. They accept whatever their employer decides to pay them. They treat income as something that happens to them rather than something they create.

This is victim thinking. This is poverty thinking. This is the thinking of someone who buried their talent.

Wealthy people think differently. They see income as a creative act. They see income as something they generate through value creation. They see income as something they control through strategic decisions about skills, industries, opportunities, and risk.

You must adopt this mindset. You are not a passive recipient of income. You are an active creator of income. You decide what you are worth. You decide what value you provide. You decide how to monetize your gifts. You decide whether to stay in low-paying work or move to high-paying work. You decide whether to rely on one income stream or build multiple streams. You decide.

God gave you gifts. God gave you abilities. God gave you time. God gave you a mind. God gave you opportunities. What you do with these resources determines your income. What you do with your income determines your wealth. What you do with your wealth determines your legacy.

The parable of the talents is not just about spiritual gifts. It is about stewardship of all resources, including your earning capacity. The servant who buried his talent was called wicked and slothful. Not unlucky. Not disadvantaged. Wicked and slothful. Those are moral judgments about character and effort.

You have abilities right now that you are not using. You have skills you are not monetizing. You have time you are wasting. You have opportunities you are ignoring. This is burying your talent. Stop burying. Start multiplying.

The Business Parallel: How Companies Think About Revenue

If your family is an economic unit, and it is, then you must think like the leadership of a successful company.

Every business begins with one question: How will we generate revenue consistently, predictably, and sustainably?

Then they ask: Who is our market? What problem do we solve? What product or service do we offer? What is our pricing model? What is our unique advantage? How do we differentiate from competition? How do we expand our revenue lines? How do we innovate? How do we scale? How do we produce income without increasing labor? How do we use research and development to increase our capacity?

Families must ask the exact same questions. You are not simply an employee hoping for a raise. You are a CEO building a revenue strategy.

Mark Cuban said it plainly: "Sales cures all." If a business knows how to generate revenue, it recovers from mistakes, survives downturns, and grows. If it cannot generate revenue, nothing else matters. The best business plan, the tightest budget, the most efficient operations mean nothing without revenue. Revenue is oxygen. Without it, the business dies.

Your household is no different. You can budget perfectly. You can cut expenses aggressively. You can eliminate waste. But if your income is insufficient, you will never build wealth. You will survive. You will maintain. You will tread water. But you will not thrive.

Revenue creates options. Revenue creates margin. Revenue creates wealth. This is why successful businesses obsess over revenue growth. They do not just accept whatever revenue comes in. They strategize about how to increase it. They innovate new products. They enter new markets. They raise prices. They improve quality. They expand distribution. They acquire competitors. They do whatever it takes to grow revenue year after year.

You must do the same. You must obsess over increasing your income. Not in a greedy way. Not in a workaholic way. In a strategic way. In a stewardship way. In a multiplication way.

Think about a corporation. A corporation does not have one product. It has product lines. It has multiple revenue streams. Apple sells phones, computers, tablets, watches, services, apps. Amazon sells retail products, cloud computing, streaming services, advertising. Microsoft sells software, cloud services, gaming, devices. Diversification protects them. If one product line declines, others compensate.

Your household needs the same diversification. If your only income is your job, you have one product. If you lose that job, your revenue goes to zero. If your industry declines, your income declines. If your company struggles, your raises stop. You are vulnerable. You are fragile. One disruption destroys you.

Corporations invest heavily in research and development. They spend millions developing new products, new technologies, new capabilities. They do this because they know current products eventually become obsolete. They must innovate or die.

You need personal research and development. You need to invest in new skills, new certifications, new knowledge, new capabilities. Your current skills will become less valuable over time. Technology changes. Industries change. Markets change. You must adapt or become obsolete.

Corporations track performance metrics obsessively. Revenue per employee. Profit margins. Customer acquisition costs. Return on investment. They measure everything because measurement reveals what works and what fails. They adjust strategy based on data, not emotions.

You need to track your income metrics. Income per hour

worked. Income per skill deployed. Income per certification earned. Income growth rate year over year. You should know these numbers. You should track them. You should use them to make strategic decisions about where to invest your time and effort.

Corporations forecast future revenue. They build three-year plans, five-year plans, ten-year plans. They set revenue targets. They work backward from those targets to determine what actions are required today to hit those numbers tomorrow.

You built financial projections in Chapter 1. Those projections include income targets. If your projection says you will earn eighty thousand dollars per year in five years, but you currently earn forty thousand, you have a forty thousand dollar gap. How will you close that gap? What skills will you develop? What certifications will you earn? What side businesses will you start? What industries will you enter? These are not vague hopes. These are strategic questions that require specific answers and concrete action plans.

This is how businesses think about revenue. This is how You, Inc. must think about income.

The Life Cycle of Income: Why You Must Build Now, Not Later

From age twenty-one to approximately age fifty, income generally rises. From fifty onward, for most people, income plateaus or declines. This is not theory. This is labor market data tracked by the Bureau of Labor Statistics over decades.

Your peak earning years are roughly age forty to fifty-five. During this window, you have maximum experience, maximum skills, maximum energy, and maximum employment value. Before this window, you are still building experience. After this window, younger workers become cheaper alternatives, age discrimination increases, and physical energy declines.

At the same time, life gets more expensive. Housing costs rise. Insurance costs rise. Medical expenses rise. Taxes rise. Education costs for children rise. Transportation costs rise. Food costs rise. Inflation compounds annually. Purchasing power erodes.

Expenses rise. Income declines. This mathematical reality destroys millions of families because they rely on a single income stream, a single employer, or a single profession. When income slows or stops, everything collapses.

The only defense is multiple streams of income, including passive income that continues to grow even when your energy, time, or employment status decline. You must build these streams now, while income is rising, not later when your capacity is shrinking.

Think about professional athletes. Athletes earn peak income during a short window, usually ages twenty-two to thirty-five. Smart athletes understand this. They save aggressively. They invest heavily. They build businesses outside sports. They create income streams that continue after their playing career ends. Athletes who do not do this go broke within five years of retirement despite earning millions during their careers.

You face a similar dynamic, just stretched over a longer timeline. Your peak earning years are finite. Your energy is finite. Your employability is finite. Your physical capacity is finite. If you do not build wealth during your peak years, you will work until you die.

Most people waste their peak earning years. They spend everything they make. They buy bigger houses. They buy nicer cars. They take expensive vacations. They lifestyle inflate their way through their forties and fifties. Then they hit sixty with no savings, no investments, no passive income, and declining job prospects. They panic. They work longer.

They work harder. They cannot retire. They cannot slow down. They are trapped.

This is preventable. This is completely avoidable. But prevention requires building multiple income streams and passive income while you are young and income is rising.

Passive income is income that continues paying when you stop working. Rental real estate pays you whether you show up or not. Dividend stocks pay you whether you work or not. Royalties from books or music pay you whether you create new work or not. Businesses with systems and employees generate profit whether you are present or not.

Active income requires your time and energy. You trade hours for dollars. When you stop working, income stops. When you get sick, income stops. When you get old, income stops. Active income is fragile.

Passive income is resilient. It continues during illness. It continues during market downturns. It continues when you want to travel. It continues when you retire. It continues when you die, providing for your family.

Your goal is to build enough passive income to cover your essential expenses. When passive income covers rent, utilities, food, insurance, and transportation, you have financial independence. You work because you want to, not because you have to. This is freedom. This is the goal.

But passive income takes years to build. Real estate requires down payments, mortgages, tenants, and time for property values to appreciate. Dividend portfolios require consistent investing over decades to reach meaningful income levels. Businesses require systems, employees, and time to become self-sustaining. Royalties require creating intellectual property and building audiences.

You cannot build these in your sixties. You must start in your twenties, thirties, or forties. The earlier you start, the more time compounding has to work. The later you start, the harder you must work to catch up.

This is why income strategy is urgent. This is why waiting is dangerous. This is why hoping your employer will take care of you is naive. Your employer has no obligation to secure your future. Your employer will replace you the moment you become too expensive or too old. This is business. This is economics. This is reality.

You must take responsibility for building multiple income streams and passive income now, during your peak earning years, so you have options later when those years end.

If You Don't Make Enough Money, Do Something About It

You cannot budget your way out of insufficient income. You cannot pray away income discipline you refuse to practice. You cannot complain your way into financial abundance.

If income is too low, you must increase it. Here is the blueprint with six steps.

1. If your job does not pay enough, seek a job that does.

There is no reward for loyalty to financial stagnation. You must not stay where your gifts are not valued. Companies love loyal employees because loyal employees accept below-market wages for years. They stay out of comfort, fear of change, or misplaced loyalty. Meanwhile, job hoppers who switch companies every two to three years average twenty to thirty percent higher lifetime earnings. The market rewards movement, not loyalty.

I have watched people stay in underpaying jobs for ten, fifteen, twenty years. They complain about their salary. They complain about lack of raises. They complain about being undervalued. But they never leave. They never interview elsewhere. They never explore options. They stay because staying is comfortable and leaving is scary. Comfort keeps you broke. Fear keeps you broke. Loyalty to a company that undervalues you keeps you broke.

If you have been in the same job for more than three years without significant raises, you are being underpaid. Update your resume. Start interviewing. Get offers. See what the market will pay you. You will likely discover you are worth twenty to forty percent more than you currently earn. Then you have a choice. Take the new offer or use it to negotiate a massive raise with your current employer. Either way, you win. But you must move. Staying guarantees continued underpayment.

2. If your industry limits your income, change industries.

Industries rise and fall. Technology disrupts. Consumer preferences shift. Regulations change. Automation eliminates jobs. Global competition drives wages down. Your industry might be dying. You must adapt.

I worked with a man who spent twenty years in print journalism. He was skilled. He was experienced. He was excellent at his craft. But print journalism died. Newspapers closed. Magazines folded. Jobs disappeared. His skills became less valuable every year. He kept hoping the industry would recover. It did not. He kept applying for fewer and fewer journalism jobs. He kept getting rejected. He finally admitted the industry was dead. He retrained. He learned digital marketing. He got hired in tech. His income doubled within two years. Twenty years of loyalty to a dying industry kept him broke. Two years in a growing industry changed his life.

You owe your industry nothing. Your industry owes you nothing. If your industry limits income, leave. Find industries that are growing, not shrinking. Tech pays more than retail. Healthcare pays more than hospitality. Finance pays more than nonprofit work. These are facts, not judgments. Different industries have different pay scales. Choose high-paying industries if income is your goal. Do not stay in low-paying industries out of passion or purpose or loyalty. Passion does not pay your mortgage. Purpose does not fund retirement. Loyalty does not build wealth. Income does.

3. Invest in new skills or certifications. Skill increases value.

Value increases income. Every certification you earn, every skill you master, every competency you develop makes you more valuable. More valuable means higher pay. This is economics.

The market pays for scarcity and value. If your skills are common, your pay is low. If your skills are rare and valuable, your pay is high. A general laborer makes fifteen dollars per hour because millions of people can do that work. A specialized welder makes forty dollars per hour because fewer people have that skill. A medical device engineer makes sixty dollars per hour because even fewer people have that knowledge. A neurosurgeon makes three hundred dollars per hour because almost nobody has that expertise. The principle is consistent: rare and valuable skills command premium pay.

You can increase your income by increasing your skill level. Take courses. Get certified. Learn new software. Master new technologies. Develop expertise in areas your industry values. Every investment in skill development pays dividends for decades.

I know people who refused to learn new skills because they were comfortable with what they already knew. They refused to learn new software because the old software worked fine. They refused to get certifications because they already had experience. They refused to adapt. The market passed them by. Younger workers with current skills got hired. They got laid off. Experience without current skills means nothing. The market does not care what you used to know. The market cares what you know now.

Invest one hour per day in skill development. One hour per day is seven hours per week. Thirty hours per month. Three hundred sixty-five hours per year. That is nine full work weeks of skill development annually. In five years, you will have completed forty-five weeks of intensive learning. Your skills will be unrecognizable compared to where you are today. Your income will reflect that growth. But you must invest the time. You must do the work. You must prioritize learning over entertainment.

4. If you will not change jobs or industries, build a side business.

Every household should have at least one additional income stream beyond employment. Side businesses provide supplemental income, test business ideas, develop entrepreneurial skills, and create paths to full-time self-employment if desired.

Side businesses start small. A few hours per week. A few hundred dollars per month. But they grow. As you gain clients, refine systems, and build reputation, income increases. Some side businesses eventually replace job income entirely. Some remain supplemental forever. Either way, they provide income diversification and reduce dependence on a single employer.

The most common objection I hear is "I don't have time for a side business." This is false. You have time. You waste time. Chapter 4 will show you exactly how to find ten to twenty hours per week you are currently wasting on entertainment, social media, and television. That time can generate five hundred to two thousand dollars per month in additional income if deployed strategically. But you must redirect time from consumption to production. You must stop watching and start building.

5. Monetize your gifts.

Your innate abilities—writing, teaching, creating, organizing, fixing, designing—are revenue generators. Everything you do well has market value. Everything people ask you for help with is something they would pay someone else to do. You can be that someone.

You are good at something. Multiple things, probably. You take these abilities for granted because they come naturally to you. They do not come naturally to everyone else. What is easy for you is hard for others. What is obvious to you is confusing to others. What takes you ten minutes takes others two hours. People will pay you for your natural abilities because your natural abilities solve their problems.

I know a woman who is exceptionally organized. She organized her own home efficiently. Friends noticed. Friends asked for help organizing their homes. She started charging fifty dollars per hour. She now makes three thousand dollars per month organizing people's homes, garages, and offices on weekends. She monetized a natural gift she did not even recognize as valuable. She thought everyone could organize like she does. They cannot. She has a skill. That skill has market value. She now captures that value.

What are you naturally good at? What do people compliment you on? What do friends and family ask you to help them with? These are clues to your monetizable gifts. List them. Research what people charge for those services. Start offering them. You will be shocked how many people will pay you for things you do effortlessly.

6. Develop a passive income strategy.

Passive income protects you when active income slows. Passive income is not truly passive. It requires upfront work. It requires initial capital. It requires systems. But once established, passive income requires minimal ongoing effort while producing consistent returns.

The goal is to build passive income streams that eventually replace your active income. When passive income covers your living expenses, you achieve financial independence. You work because you want to, not because you have to. Most people never reach this point because they never start building passive income. They work for forty years, earn active income only, and retire on Social Security. They spent decades working but built nothing that pays them when they stop working. This is tragic. This is avoidable.

Start small. Invest in dividend stocks. Buy one rental property. Create one digital product. Write one book. Build one small business. These are seeds. They produce small returns initially. But they grow. Dividends compound. Property values appreciate. Digital products sell repeatedly. Royalties accumulate. Businesses scale. In twenty years, these small seeds become forests of income-producing assets. But you must plant seeds today. You cannot plant seeds in twenty years and harvest immediately. Passive income requires time. Start now.

Every strategy I just described requires the same thing: action. You must act. You must move. You must change. You must try. Most people will read this section and do nothing. They will agree with everything I said. They will recognize their situation in every example. They will acknowledge their income is insufficient. Then they will change nothing. They will stay in the same underpaying job. They will stay in the same declining industry. They will refuse to learn new skills. They will never start a side business. They will never monetize their gifts. They will never build passive income. They will stay broke for decades because they refuse to act.

You will act. You will pick one strategy from this section. You will implement it this week. You will start. You will build momentum. You will increase your income. You will create options. You will build wealth. But you must start. You must act. You must do what broke people will not do.

The Top Ten Side Hustles Most Americans Can Do

Three major studies—McKinsey, Bankrate, and Self Financial—confirm that between twenty-seven and forty-five percent of United States adults already operate a side hustle. This is not fringe behavior. This is mainstream economics. Nearly half of working Americans supplement their primary income with additional revenue streams. You should too.

Based on labor market data, accessibility research, and demand analysis, here are the top ten side hustles ninety percent of adults can perform with low startup costs and high practicality. These are not get-rich-quick schemes. These are legitimate businesses people operate successfully right now while working full-time jobs.

1. Freelance Writing, Editing, or Ghostwriting

Every business needs content. Websites need copy. Blogs need articles. Companies need white papers. Executives need speeches. Authors need ghostwriters. Marketing departments need email campaigns. The demand for written content is infinite.

You do not need a journalism degree. You do not need perfect grammar. You need the ability to communicate clearly and the willingness to learn. Writing is a skill you develop through practice, not through credentials. Clients care about results, not degrees.

Freelance writers earn twenty-five to one hundred fifty

dollars per hour depending on specialization and experience. New writers start at the lower end. Experienced writers with specialized knowledge command premium rates. Technical writers, medical writers, and financial writers earn more than general content writers because their knowledge is rarer.

Start on platforms like Upwork, Fiverr, or Contently. Create a profile. Apply for beginner-level jobs. Build a portfolio. Get reviews. Raise your rates. After twenty to thirty completed projects, you have enough reputation to attract clients directly. Direct clients mean no platform fees and higher take-home pay.

The barrier to entry is low. The income potential is high. The flexibility is total. You work when you want, where you want, as much as you want. Writing is one of the most accessible side hustles available.

2. Virtual Assistant and Administrative Support

Entrepreneurs, executives, and small business owners need administrative help. They need someone to manage calendars, book travel, respond to emails, organize files, schedule meetings, handle customer service, process invoices, and manage a thousand small tasks that consume their time.

Virtual assistants work remotely. You need basic office skills, reliable internet, a computer, and organizational ability. Most virtual assistant tasks require no specialized training. If you have worked in an office, you already have these skills.

Virtual assistants earn fifteen to forty dollars per hour. Entry-level assistants start around fifteen to twenty dollars per hour. Experienced assistants with specialized skills—bookkeeping, social media management, project management—earn thirty to forty dollars per hour or more.

Find clients on platforms like Belay, Time Etc, or Fancy Hands. These companies match virtual assistants with clients. You apply, get approved, and they assign you work. Alternatively, pitch directly to small business owners in your network or local area. Most small businesses need administrative support but cannot afford a full-time employee. You become their part-time solution.

The work is steady. The hours are flexible. The skills are transferable. Virtual assistant work provides reliable supplemental income with minimal startup costs.

3. Online Tutoring

Parents pay for academic help. Students need tutoring in math, science, English, reading, test prep, and foreign languages. The market is enormous. The demand is consistent. The pay is good.

Online tutoring requires subject knowledge and the ability to explain concepts clearly. You do not need teaching credentials for most platforms. You need to demonstrate competency in your subject area and pass basic background checks.

Tutors earn twenty to sixty dollars per hour depending on subject and level. Elementary tutoring pays twenty to thirty dollars per hour. High school tutoring pays thirty to forty-five dollars per hour. College tutoring and test prep pay forty-five to sixty dollars per hour or more.

Join platforms like Tutor.com, Wyzant, Chegg Tutors, or VIPKid for teaching English to international students. Create a profile. Set your rates. Students book sessions. You teach via video chat. The platforms handle payment processing and scheduling.

Alternatively, advertise locally. Post flyers at libraries, coffee shops, and community centers. Join local parenting groups on social media. Word of mouth spreads quickly when you deliver results. Many successful tutors build local client bases and leave platforms entirely to avoid commission fees.

Tutoring scales with your available time. Tutor five hours per week for extra income. Tutor twenty hours per week for substantial income. The flexibility allows you to control exactly how much you work and earn.

4. Graphic Design

Every business needs visual content. Logos, social media graphics, website banners, marketing materials, business cards, presentations, infographics, and advertisements all require design work. Small businesses especially need affordable design help.

You do not need formal design training. Tools like Canva, Adobe Express, and Figma make professional-quality design accessible to beginners. YouTube tutorials teach design principles for free. Practice builds skill faster than education.

Beginner designers earn twenty-five to fifty dollars per project. Experienced designers earn seventy-five to two hundred dollars per project depending on complexity. Logo design, brand identity packages, and website design command premium rates.

Start on Fiverr or 99designs. Create a portfolio with sample designs. Offer competitive introductory rates. Get five to ten completed projects with good reviews. Then raise your rates. Many designers quickly move to direct clients through Instagram, personal websites, or referrals. Direct clients eliminate platform fees and increase profit margins.

Design work is project-based. You can work on your schedule. Complete projects during evenings and weekends. Build a client base slowly while maintaining your full-time job. Eventually, some designers transition to full-time freelance work as their client roster grows.

5. Social Media Management

Small businesses need social media presence but lack time or expertise to manage it. They need someone to create content, schedule posts, respond to comments, run advertisements, and grow their following. This is where you come in.

Social media management requires no formal education. You need familiarity with platforms, basic design skills, copywriting ability, and consistency. If you use social media personally, you have foundational knowledge. The rest you learn through practice and free online resources.

Social media managers earn three hundred to two thousand dollars per month per client depending on scope. Managing one platform for a small business pays three hundred to five hundred dollars monthly. Managing multiple platforms with content creation and advertising pays one thousand to two thousand dollars monthly.

Start by offering services to local businesses. Walk into small shops, restaurants, salons, or service businesses. Look at their social media. If it is dormant or poorly managed, offer to help. Show them what you would do differently. Propose a monthly package. Many small business owners recognize they need social media help but do not know where to find it. You become their solution.

Managing three to five clients generates fifteen hundred to seven thousand five hundred dollars in monthly recurring revenue. This is substantial supplemental income. The work takes ten to fifteen hours per week once systems are established. The income is predictable. Clients typically stay for months or years. This is one of the best recurring-revenue side hustles available.

6. Remote Customer Service or Chat Support

Major companies constantly hire remote customer service representatives. Airlines, banks, retailers, tech companies, and service providers all need customer support. Many offer evening and weekend shifts perfect for side income.

Customer service work requires patience, communication

skills, and basic computer competency. You answer phone calls, respond to chat messages, resolve customer issues, and process simple transactions. Training is provided. No specialized knowledge is required.

Remote customer service pays twelve to twenty-five dollars per hour. Entry positions start around twelve to fifteen dollars per hour. Technical support and specialized support roles pay eighteen to twenty-five dollars per hour.

Companies like Amazon, Apple, American Express, Hilton, and hundreds of others hire remote customer service workers. Search "remote customer service" on Indeed, FlexJobs, or company career pages. Apply directly. Most positions are part-time with flexible schedules. You choose your hours based on availability.

This is straightforward supplemental income. No business building required. No client acquisition needed. No marketing necessary. You apply, get hired, work your scheduled shifts, and get paid. The simplicity makes this attractive for people who want extra income without entrepreneurial complexity.

7. Selling Digital Products

Digital products are items you create once and sell infinitely. Templates, eBooks, printables, courses, stock photos, graphics, spreadsheets, checklists, planners, guides. Create them once. List them on platforms like Etsy, Gumroad, or Teachable. Earn money while you sleep.

Digital products require upfront work but generate passive income afterward. A budget spreadsheet template takes five hours to create. List it for ten dollars. Sell it three hundred times over two years. That is three thousand dollars from five hours of work. That is six hundred dollars per hour. This is the power of digital products.

Popular digital products include:

- Budget spreadsheets and financial planners
- Resume and cover letter templates
- Business plan templates
- Social media content calendars
- Meal planning templates
- Workout plans and fitness guides
- eBooks on specialized topics
- Online courses teaching skills
- Printable wall art and planners
- Stock photos and graphics

Research what sells on Etsy or Gumroad in your area of knowledge. Create similar products with your unique angle. Price them between five and fifty dollars depending on complexity. Market them through social media, Pinterest, or paid ads. Sales compound over time as more people discover your products.

The initial sales are slow. Months one through three generate minimal revenue. Months four through twelve generate increasing revenue as your product library grows and search rankings improve. Year two and beyond generate substantial passive income as you have twenty to fifty products all selling continuously.

Digital products require patience and consistent creation. But they scale infinitely. Physical products require inventory and shipping. Services require your time. Digital products require neither. You create once and sell forever. This is one of the most scalable side hustles available.

8. E-commerce and Print-on-Demand

E-commerce traditionally required inventory, warehousing, and shipping logistics. Print-on-demand eliminates these barriers. You design products. Upload designs to platforms.

They handle production, inventory, shipping, and customer service. You collect profit.

Print-on-demand works for t-shirts, mugs, phone cases, posters, tote bags, notebooks, and more. Platforms like Printful, Printify, Redbubble, and Teespring integrate with Etsy, Shopify, or Amazon. You create designs. Customers order. The platform produces and ships. You earn the difference between wholesale cost and retail price.

Profit margins are smaller than traditional e-commerce. A t-shirt might generate five to ten dollars profit per sale. But you have zero upfront costs. No inventory risk. No shipping headaches. You focus entirely on design and marketing.

Successful print-on-demand sellers create niche designs for specific audiences. Generic designs get lost in competition. Specific designs for specific groups—dog lovers, nurses, specific hobbies, specific professions—perform better. The more specific, the less competition, the higher the conversion rate.

This side hustle requires design skills and marketing ability. The design tools are accessible. The marketing takes experimentation. Some sellers generate two hundred to five hundred dollars monthly. Some generate five thousand to ten thousand dollars monthly. Scale depends on design quality, niche selection, and marketing consistency.

9. Home and Gig Services

Local service businesses always need workers. Cleaning, organizing, handyman work, lawn care, moving help, junk removal, pet sitting, dog walking, errand services. These are labor-based services with immediate demand and simple startup.

Service businesses require basic skills, reliability, and willingness to work. Most require minimal equipment. Cleaning requires supplies. Lawn care requires a mower. Moving help requires strength and a vehicle. Pet sitting requires trustworthiness. The barriers are low.

Service providers earn fifteen to forty dollars per hour depending on service. Cleaning pays twenty to thirty-five dollars per hour. Handyman work pays thirty to fifty dollars per hour. Pet sitting pays fifteen to twenty-five dollars per visit. Dog walking pays fifteen to twenty dollars per walk.

Find clients through local Facebook groups, Nextdoor, Craigslist, TaskRabbit, or Thumbtack. List your services. Respond to requests. Build reputation through reviews. Word of mouth generates additional clients quickly in local service businesses.

Service work is straightforward. Show up. Do the work. Get paid. No complex business models. No steep learning curves. Just reliable labor for fair compensation. This suits people who prefer hands-on work over digital work.

10. Coaching or Consulting

You know things other people want to learn. Career skills, life skills, business skills, relationship skills, parenting skills, financial skills, health skills. Your knowledge has value. People will pay you to teach them what you know.

Coaching requires expertise in a specific area and the ability to guide others. You do not need certifications for most coaching niches. You need results in your own life and the ability to help others achieve similar results. Life coaches, career coaches, business coaches, health coaches, and relationship coaches all operate successfully without formal credentials.

Coaches earn fifty to three hundred dollars per hour depending on niche and reputation. Beginner coaches charge fifty to one hundred dollars per session. Experienced coaches with proven results charge one hundred fifty to three hundred dollars per session or more.

Start by coaching friends, family, or colleagues for free. Build testimonials. Refine your process. Then start charging. Offer introductory rates to attract initial clients. Raise rates as demand increases. Most coaches fill their schedules quickly once word spreads about their effectiveness.

Coaching scales with your available time. Coach three clients per week for extra income. Coach ten clients per week for substantial income. The work is fulfilling because you help people achieve meaningful goals. The income is strong because transformation is valuable.

The Top Ten Passive Income Streams

Active income requires your time and energy. Passive income continues paying when you stop working. Building passive income is the most important financial work you will ever do. Passive income buys time. Passive income buys freedom. Passive income buys options.

These are the ten most accessible passive income streams that resist inflation and do not depend on physical labor. Some require capital. Some require time. All require upfront work. But once established, they generate income with minimal ongoing effort.

1. Rental Real Estate (Long-Term)

Real estate has created more millionaires than any other investment vehicle in American history. Rental properties generate monthly cash flow while property values appreciate over decades. You profit twice—from rent payments and from property value increases.

Real estate requires capital for down payments. Conventional mortgages require fifteen to twenty percent down. FHA loans require three and a half percent down. Down payments on a two hundred thousand dollar property range from seven thousand to forty thousand dollars. This is accessible for people who save consistently.

Rental properties generate cash flow after mortgage, taxes, insurance, and maintenance. A property generating three hundred dollars monthly cash flow produces thirty-six hundred dollars annually. Ten properties produce thirty-six thousand dollars annually. This is substantial passive income.

Property values appreciate at roughly three to five percent annually on average. A two hundred thousand dollar property becomes three hundred twenty-five thousand dollars in fifteen years at four percent appreciation. You profited one hundred twenty-five thousand dollars just from appreciation. Add fifteen years of rent payments minus expenses, and total returns often exceed two hundred percent over fifteen years.

Real estate is not truly passive. Properties require management. Tenants require screening. Repairs happen. Vacancies occur. But property managers handle day-to-day operations for eight to ten percent of monthly rent. You collect profits while managers handle work. This is as passive as real estate gets.

Start with one property. Save the down payment. Buy a property. Rent it. Manage or hire management. Use cash flow to save for property two. Repeat. Build a portfolio slowly over years. This is how ordinary people build seven-figure real estate portfolios. One property. Then two. Then five. Then ten. Compounding works in real estate just like in stocks. But you must start.

2. Short-Term Rentals and Airbnb

Short-term rentals generate higher income than long-term rentals but require more management. Airbnb, VRBO, and similar platforms allow you to rent properties by the night or week instead of by the month or year.

Short-term rentals in desirable locations often produce

two to three times the income of long-term rentals. A property that rents for fifteen hundred dollars monthly long-term might generate three thousand to four thousand dollars monthly as a short-term rental. The income difference is substantial.

The tradeoffs are higher management requirements and more regulations. Short-term rentals require furnishing, cleaning between guests, guest communication, and compliance with local regulations. Many cities restrict or ban short-term rentals. Research local laws before pursuing this strategy.

Some investors buy properties specifically for short-term rental income. Others rent out spare bedrooms or vacation homes when not using them. Both approaches generate income. The key is location. Properties near tourist destinations, business districts, or event venues command premium nightly rates. Properties in random suburbs do not.

Short-term rentals work well for people who enjoy hospitality and property management. If you hate dealing with people or managing details, long-term rentals are better. But if you want maximum income from real estate, short-term rentals often deliver higher returns.

3. Dividend-Paying Stocks and ETFs

Dividend stocks pay you quarterly just for owning them. Companies distribute a portion of profits to shareholders. You buy shares. You receive dividend payments. You reinvest dividends to buy more shares. Your income grows over time.

Dividend yields range from two to six percent annually. A one hundred thousand dollar dividend portfolio yielding four percent generates four thousand dollars annually, or about three hundred thirty-three dollars monthly. A five hundred thousand dollar portfolio generates twenty thousand dollars annually, or about sixteen hundred sixty-seven dollars monthly.

Building a dividend portfolio requires consistent investing over decades. You cannot save one hundred thousand dollars overnight. But you can save five thousand dollars this year. Then five thousand next year. Then every year for twenty years. Twenty years of five thousand dollar annual investments at eight percent growth creates two hundred forty-five thousand dollars. At a four percent dividend yield, that generates nine thousand eight hundred dollars annually in passive income.

Dividend investing requires patience. Early years produce minimal income. A five thousand dollar portfolio yielding four percent generates only two hundred dollars annually. That feels insignificant. But you are building. Decade two produces significant income. Decade three produces substantial income. Decade four produces enough income to potentially replace employment income.

Most people quit dividend investing because early results are small. They do not see the point of two hundred dollars per year. They miss the compounding. That two hundred dollars reinvested buys more shares. Those shares generate more dividends. Those dividends buy more shares. The cycle compounds. In thirty years, that initial five thousand dollar investment generates passive income forever. But you must start. You must stay invested. You must let compounding work.

4. High-Yield Savings and Money Market Funds

High-yield savings accounts and money market funds are not wealth-building tools. They are wealth-preservation tools. They generate low returns—currently around four to five percent annually—but provide safety and liquidity.

A fifty thousand dollar emergency fund in a high-yield

savings account earning four and a half percent generates twenty-two hundred fifty dollars annually. That is one hundred eighty-seven dollars monthly. Not substantial. But not nothing. Your emergency fund should work for you while sitting safely accessible.

Compare this to traditional savings accounts paying zero point five percent. That same fifty thousand dollars earns only two hundred fifty dollars annually in a traditional account. That is twenty-one dollars monthly. You are losing two thousand dollars annually by using a traditional savings account instead of a high-yield account. Switch accounts. Earn the difference. This is free money.

Money market funds function similarly. They invest in ultra-safe short-term securities. They pay slightly higher rates than high-yield savings. They are liquid. You can withdraw anytime. They serve as parking spots for cash waiting for investment opportunities while earning modest returns.

These are not exciting passive income streams. But they are smart. Your emergency fund exists. It should earn something. High-yield savings and money market funds ensure it does.

5. Digital Products

We covered digital products as an active side hustle. But digital products transition to passive income over time. Create products once. Sell them forever. Minimal ongoing effort required.

A library of twenty digital products generates passive income continuously. One product might sell ten copies monthly at fifteen dollars each. That is one hundred fifty dollars monthly from one product. Twenty products each selling ten copies monthly generates three thousand dollars monthly. That is thirty-six thousand dollars annually. This is meaningful passive income.

The work is frontend-loaded. Creating twenty quality products takes months. But once created, they sell indefinitely. You wake up to sales notifications. You did nothing yesterday. You earned money anyway. This is passive income.

Successful digital product creators build product libraries over years. They create consistently. They market systematically. They grow slowly. But they build income streams that pay them for years after creation. This is scalable passive income with zero inventory costs and zero ongoing production costs.

6. Licensing and Royalties

Create intellectual property. License it. Earn royalties. Books, music, photography, artwork, patents, trademarks, courses. Create once. License repeatedly. Earn forever.

Authors earn royalties from book sales. Musicians earn royalties from streaming and licensing. Photographers earn royalties from stock photo sales. Course creators earn royalties from course sales. Patent holders earn royalties from product licensing. Trademark owners earn royalties from brand licensing.

Royalties compound over time as your intellectual property library grows. One book generates modest royalties. Ten books generate substantial royalties. Fifty books generate life-changing royalties. But you must create. You must publish. You must build the library.

Most creative people create once and move on. They write one book. They record one album. They create one course. They never build a library. They never achieve royalty income scale. You must create systematically. One book this year. Two books next year. Three the year after. In ten years, you have twenty books all generating royalties continuously. This is how writers, musicians, and creators achieve financial independence. Not from one hit. From consistent creation over years.

7. Businesses That Operate Without Your Daily Labor

The ultimate passive income is a business that generates profit without your presence. This requires systems, employees, and processes that function independently. You built it. Now it runs without you.

Most businesses require the owner's constant involvement. The business is a job, not an asset. When the owner stops working, income stops. These are not passive income machines. These are self-employment.

True passive businesses are rare. They require exceptional systems, strong management, and clear processes. They take years to build. But they are possible. Car washes, laundromats, vending machine routes, storage facilities, online businesses with fulfillment outsourcing, franchise ownership with manager operators. These businesses generate cash flow without daily owner involvement.

Building passive businesses is advanced strategy. Start with simpler passive income streams first. But understand the goal. The ultimate passive income is owning assets—real estate, businesses, intellectual property—that pay you without consuming your time. This is wealth. This is freedom. This is the goal.

8. Peer-to-Peer Lending and REITs

Peer-to-peer lending platforms allow you to lend money to borrowers and earn interest. Returns average five to nine percent annually. Higher returns than bonds. More risk than bonds. But diversification across hundreds of loans reduces individual default risk.

REITs (Real Estate Investment Trusts) allow you to invest

in real estate without buying properties. REITs own commercial properties, apartments, hotels, storage facilities. They distribute ninety percent of profits to shareholders. You buy REIT shares like stocks. You earn dividends from real estate without property management headaches.

Both strategies provide income diversification. You are not buying more stocks. You are buying different asset classes with different risk profiles. Diversification protects you during market volatility. When stocks decline, real estate might hold steady. When bonds decline, peer-to-peer lending might generate returns. Diversification is wisdom.

9. Renting Assets

You own things. Other people need those things temporarily. Rent them out. Earn income.

Cars sit unused. Rent them on Turo. Equipment sits in garages. Rent it on Fat Llama. Tools sit in sheds. Rent them locally. Spare rooms sit empty. Rent them on Airbnb. Parking spaces sit unused. Rent them on SpotHero. Storage spaces sit empty. Rent them on Neighbor.

Every idle asset is potential income. The asset already exists. You already own it. Renting generates income from existing resources. This is capital efficiency. Your money is working instead of sitting idle.

The returns vary by asset. Renting a car generates two hundred to six hundred dollars monthly. Renting equipment generates fifty to two hundred dollars monthly. Renting storage space generates one hundred to three hundred dollars monthly. Every rental adds to total passive income. Multiple rental assets compound into meaningful monthly income.

10. Content Monetization

Create content. Build an audience. Monetize attention.

YouTube ads, blog ads, podcast sponsorships, affiliate marketing, membership communities. Create valuable content. Attract viewers. Earn revenue.

Content creation requires consistency over years. Early months generate zero income. You create for free. You build an audience slowly. But audiences compound. One hundred subscribers become one thousand. One thousand becomes ten thousand. Ten thousand becomes one hundred thousand. Revenue scales with audience size.

YouTube pays one to five dollars per thousand views depending on niche and advertiser demand. A channel generating one hundred thousand views monthly earns one hundred to five hundred dollars monthly from ads. Add affiliate income and sponsorships, and total revenue reaches one thousand to three thousand dollars monthly.

Podcasters earn from sponsorships. Sponsors pay twenty to fifty dollars per thousand downloads. A podcast generating ten thousand downloads monthly earns two hundred to five hundred dollars per episode from sponsors.

Bloggers earn from ads and affiliate commissions. Blogs with fifty thousand monthly visitors earn five hundred to two thousand dollars monthly from display ads. Add affiliate product recommendations, and earnings reach two thousand to five thousand dollars monthly.

Content monetization is passive income after the content library is built. Old videos continue generating views. Old blog posts continue attracting visitors. Old podcast episodes continue being downloaded. You created once. You earn forever. This is scalable passive income.

Your Personal Research and Development Plan

Every great business has a research and development department. Most families do not. This is where your income stagnates or transforms.

Research and development means investing in your future capacity. Companies spend billions developing new products, new technologies, new capabilities. They do this because current products eventually become obsolete. They must innovate or die.

You need personal research and development. You need to invest in new skills, new certifications, new knowledge, new capabilities. Your current skills will become less valuable over time. Technology changes. Industries change. Markets change. You must adapt or become obsolete.

Most people stop learning after they finish formal education. They get a degree. They get a job. They stop learning. They coast on existing knowledge for decades. Then they wonder why their income stagnates while others advance. The answer is simple: they stopped growing while others kept learning.

Your personal research and development plan should include seven steps:

1. Identify your top five skills.

Write them down. What are you exceptionally good at? What do you do better than most people? These are your current revenue-generating assets. Maintain them. Sharpen them. Stay current. Do not let your core skills become outdated.

2. Identify your top five interests.

What fascinates you? What would you study even if nobody paid you? Interest fuels sustained learning. You cannot force yourself to learn things you hate. But you will voluntarily invest hundreds of hours learning things that interest you. Interest is a strategic advantage.

3. Identify your top five marketable abilities.

What can you do that people will pay for? Skills plus market demand equals income. Skills without market demand equals hobby. You need both. Find the intersection of what you can do and what people will pay for. Focus there.

4. Choose three skills to develop in the next twelve months.

Not ten skills. Three. Focus is everything. Most people try to learn too many things simultaneously. They make minimal progress on everything. You will master three skills this year. Deep competency in three areas beats surface knowledge in ten areas.

5. Complete two certifications annually.

Certifications signal competency. Employers value them. Clients value them. The market values them. Certifications separate you from people with equal experience but no formal validation. Invest one hundred to five hundred dollars per certification. Invest fifty to one hundred hours of study time per certification. Earn two certifications annually. In five years, you have ten certifications. Your value to employers and clients increases dramatically.

6. Create one new revenue stream every year.

This year, start a side hustle. Next year, build passive income. The year after, launch a second side hustle. Each new revenue stream diversifies your income. Each new stream reduces dependence on your primary job. In ten years, you have ten revenue streams. If one fails, nine remain. This is resilience. This is security. This is wealth.

7. Build one passive income asset every twenty-four to thirty-six months.

Buy rental property every two to three years. Build a dividend portfolio consistently. Create digital product libraries. Develop royalty-generating intellectual property. One passive asset now is good. Five passive assets in ten years is better. Ten passive assets in twenty years is financial independence. But you must start. You must build systematically. You must stay committed for decades.

This is strategic income expansion. This is personal research and development. This is how ordinary people build extraordinary income over time. Not through luck. Not through inheritance. Through systematic skill development, strategic income diversification, and patient wealth building.

Most people will read this section and do nothing. They will not identify their skills. They will not develop new capabilities. They will not earn certifications. They will not create new revenue streams. They will not build passive assets. They will coast for decades wondering why they never advance financially. The answer is simple: they refused to invest in their own development.

You will invest. You will grow. You will build. You will transform your income capacity over the next decade. This is research and development. This is how you win.

The Income Expansion Framework

Here is your complete income expansion framework. This is your roadmap from where you are now to financial independence.

Five levels. Each level builds on the previous level. Master each level before advancing to the next.

- Level 1: Job Income (Primary Revenue)

Your job is your foundation. Master it. Increase your skill. Position for advancement. Become the most valuable employee in your department. Get raises. Get promotions. Maximize your primary income source before adding secondary sources.

Do not skip this level. Do not ignore your job while building side income. Your job is your largest revenue stream. Optimize it first. A ten percent raise at your job might generate more income than starting a side business. Do not neglect easy money pursuing harder money.

Stay at Level 1 until you have maximized your job income through raises, promotions, or job changes. Then move to Level 2.

- Level 2: Side Income (Active Revenue Streams)

Add one active side hustle. Choose from the ten side hustles listed earlier. Commit to it for twelve months. Build it to five hundred to two thousand dollars monthly. Prove to yourself you can create income outside employment.

This is psychological as much as economic. You learn you are not dependent on your employer. You learn you can generate income independently. You learn you have monetizable skills. This confidence is valuable. This confidence leads to bigger risks and bigger rewards later.

Stay at Level 2 until your side income is consistent and stable. Then move to Level 3.

- Level 3: Passive Income (Investment Revenue Streams)

Build your first passive income asset. Buy rental property. Build a dividend portfolio. Create digital products. Start small. A five thousand dollar investment in dividend stocks. A down payment on one rental property. A library of ten digital products. Small beginnings lead to large outcomes over time.

The goal at Level 3 is proving passive income works. You experience earning money without trading hours for dollars. You see dividends deposit into your account. You see rent payments arrive monthly. You see digital product sales notifications. This is transformational. This changes how you think about money and time.

Stay at Level 3 until your passive income exceeds five hundred dollars monthly. Then move to Level 4.

- Level 4: Scalable Income (Automated and Systematized Revenue)

Build businesses or income streams that grow without proportional increases in your time. Hire employees. Build systems. Create processes. Automate operations. Your income scales while your time investment does not.

This is advanced strategy. Most people never reach Level 4. They stay in Level 2 trading time for money indefinitely. Level 4 requires systems thinking, delegation ability, and trust in processes. Not everyone develops these capabilities. But those who do build income that scales exponentially.

Examples of Level 4 income: businesses with employees, online businesses with fulfillment outsourcing, large passive income portfolios generating substantial monthly income, multiple rental properties managed by property managers, large digital product libraries generating consistent sales.

Stay at Level 4 until your passive and scalable income combined equals fifty percent of your employment income. Then move to Level 5.

- Level 5: Legacy Income (Long-Term Wealth and Generational Assets)

Build wealth that lasts beyond your lifetime. Real estate portfolios worth millions. Investment portfolios generating six figures annually. Businesses that run independently and can be sold or passed to heirs. Intellectual property generating royalties for decades. Trusts and estate plans ensuring wealth transfers efficiently to the next generation.

Level 5 is not about earning more money. You have enough. Level 5 is about preserving wealth, growing wealth, and transferring wealth. Tax optimization becomes important. Estate planning becomes important. Wealth protection becomes important. You shift from accumulation to preservation and distribution.

Most people never reach Level 5. Most people never build wealth large enough to require preservation strategies. But you will. You will build through Levels 1 through 4 systematically. You will reach Level 5 in twenty to thirty years. Then you will face different problems—good problems—about how to manage substantial wealth.

This is the economic life cycle of the wise. Five levels. Each level builds capacity for the next level. Progress through them sequentially. Do not skip levels. Do not rush. Build foundation before building height. The system works if you work the system.

The Spiritual Law of Income

"Commit your work to the Lord, and your plans will be established."

God establishes plans rooted in diligence, growth, and purpose. Not passivity. Not hoping. Not wishing. Diligence, growth, and purpose.

You commit your work by working with excellence. You

commit your income strategy by executing with discipline. You commit your wealth building by acting with wisdom. Then God establishes your plans. God blesses productive effort directed toward righteous purposes.

This is not prosperity gospel. This is not "name it and claim it." This is biblical stewardship. God gives gifts. You multiply them through faithful work. The multiplication honors God. The results bless your family. The process builds character. The outcome creates options to serve others.

Your income is not just about you. Your income supports your family. Your income funds your church. Your income helps your community. Your income creates jobs when you hire others. Your income blesses the economy when you spend wisely. Your income builds generational wealth when you invest faithfully.

Increasing income is not greed. Increasing income is stewardship. You are multiplying the talent God gave you. This honors Him. This fulfills your purpose. This advances the Kingdom.

Work hard. Work smart. Work strategically. Build multiple income streams. Create passive income. Invest for decades. Leave a legacy. This is faithful stewardship. This is God-honoring economics. This is how you multiply your talent instead of burying it.

The Bridge to Allocation

You now understand income. You recognize income as foundational. You see income as strategic. You know how to increase it, diversify it, and scale it.

But income without allocation is chaos. Income without budget is waste. Income without system is vulnerability. You need both. You need strong income and wise allocation. They work together. They must be balanced. They create wealth when combined.

Chapter 4 will teach you allocation. You will learn where your income should go. You will learn percentages for housing, transportation, food, savings, debt elimination, and every other category. You will learn how to allocate every dollar before the month begins. You will learn zero-based budgeting. You will learn cash envelopes. You will learn automation.

But allocation only works when income is sufficient. If your income is too low, allocation cannot fix that. You must fix income first. Then allocation optimizes that income. Then savings accumulates. Then investments grow. Then wealth builds.

You just completed the income work. You understand revenue strategy. You know how You, Inc. generates power. Now you will learn how You, Inc. allocates power. Income creates. Allocation directs. Together they build wealth that lasts.

Turn the page. Learn allocation. Build your complete financial system.

CHAPTER 4
THE ALLOCATION SYSTEM – YOUR MONEY BLUEPRINT

Income creates opportunity, but allocation determines outcomes.

This is where many households lose control—not because they don't earn, but because they don't assign. Money that is not given direction will always find its own destination, and that destination is usually convenience. Left unmanaged, income becomes lifestyle. Left ungoverned, surplus disappears.

Allocation is not restriction. Allocation is authority.

When you allocate your money, you are deciding in advance what matters. You are declaring priorities before emotion enters the room. You are removing negotiation from the moment of temptation. In business, this is called planning. In life, it is called maturity.

This chapter introduces your allocation system—the blueprint that turns income into progress.

The Spiritual Foundation: Order and Stewardship

God works through order, not confusion. First Corinthians 14:40 states: "But all things should be done decently and in order." This is not merely a principle for worship services. This is a principle for all of life, including your finances.

When your money is disordered, your life is disordered. When you have no plan for where money goes, you cannot know if you are managing it well. When you cannot manage well, you cannot multiply. When you cannot multiply, you fail the basic test of stewardship.

The parable of the talents in Matthew 25 teaches allocation before it teaches multiplication. The master gave each servant a specific amount. He did not dump all the money in a pile and tell them to figure it out. He allocated. Five talents to one. Two talents to another. One talent to the third. The allocation itself was strategic. The master understood each servant's capacity and allocated accordingly.

Then the master expected multiplication. But multiplication could only happen because allocation happened first. The servants knew exactly what they had been given. They knew exactly what they were responsible for. They allocated their time, effort, and resources to multiply what they received. Clear allocation enabled faithful stewardship.

You are both the master and the servant in your financial life. You receive income from God—through your labor, your gifts, your opportunities. You must allocate that income strategically. You must assign every dollar a purpose. You must deploy resources in an order that honors God, protects your future, and sustains your present. This is stewardship. This is order. This is how you multiply your talent instead of burying it.

The Business Foundation: Cash Flow Management

Every profitable business tracks cash flow obsessively. Revenue is important. Profit is important. But cash flow determines survival. A business can be profitable on paper and still collapse if cash flow is mismanaged. They have revenue. They have customers. They have contracts. But they run out of actual cash to pay suppliers, employees, and rent. The business dies not from lack of sales but from lack of cash-flow discipline.

Businesses survive through strategic allocation. They allocate cash in a specific sequence. They pay critical expenses first—payroll, rent, suppliers. They allocate reserves second—emergency funds, operating capital, growth investments. They allocate discretionary spending last—office perks, bonuses, upgrades. This sequence is not arbitrary. This sequence ensures survival first, stability second, and growth third.

You, Inc. operates under the same principles. Your household is an economic unit. Your income is your revenue. Your expenses are your operating costs. Your savings and investments are your retained earnings and capital allocation. If you manage cash flow like a failing business—spending randomly, hoping something is left over, reacting instead of planning—you will fail like a failing business.

But if you manage cash flow like a successful business—allocating strategically, prioritizing survival and stability, protecting reserves, deploying capital intelligently—you will build wealth like a successful business builds enterprise value.

The allocation system you will learn in this chapter mirrors how the most disciplined corporations manage cash. You will allocate in a hierarchy. You will fund critical categories first. You will protect reserves. You will limit discretionary spending to what remains after essentials and wealth-building are funded. This is not restriction. This is intelligent resource management. This is how businesses and households survive, stabilize, and ultimately thrive.

The Behavioral Foundation: Pre-Commitment and Automation

Human willpower fails. You intend to save money. You plan to spend wisely. You commit to staying within limits. Then temptation arrives. You see something you want. You justify the purchase. You spend money you intended to save. Your plan collapses. This pattern repeats monthly. You start with good intentions. You end with empty accounts.

Behavioral economics teaches that the best financial decisions are made before emotions are involved. Pre-commitment works. Automation works. Default settings work. When you allocate money before the month begins, you make rational decisions while calm and focused. When you automate transfers, you remove the opportunity for emotional spending. When you create systems that run without daily willpower, you eliminate the primary cause of budget failure.

This is why the allocation system includes automation. This is why you assign every dollar a job before you receive income. This is why you move money to savings the day you get paid. This is why you use cash envelopes for variable spending. These are not arbitrary rules. These are behavioral guardrails that protect you from your own impulses.

The allocation system works with human nature, not against it. You will feel tempted to overspend. You will want things you cannot afford. You will rationalize bad decisions. The system anticipates this. The system removes opportunities to fail. The system makes good decisions automatic and bad decisions difficult. This is behavioral design. This is how you build discipline that lasts.

The Allocation Hierarchy: The Order That Builds Wealth

The Power Budget uses a specific allocation sequence. This sequence is non-negotiable. This sequence is what separates this system from random budgeting advice. Most budget systems treat all expenses equally. They allocate money to categories without priority or purpose. Rent, groceries, entertainment, savings—everything gets funded simultaneously with no hierarchy.

This approach fails because it does not reflect reality. Not all expenses are equally important. Not all financial obligations carry the same weight. A system that treats your Netflix subscription the same as your emergency fund is a system designed to keep you broke.

The Power Budget allocation hierarchy is:

- First: God and Generosity

If you believe your income comes from God, you honor Him first. Tithes, offerings, and intentional generosity are not afterthoughts. They are first fruits. Proverbs 3:9 commands: "Honor the Lord with your wealth and with the first fruits of all your produce." This is not a suggestion. This is a command. You give first, before you see what remains.

- Second: Yourself (Savings and Wealth Building)

Pay yourself second. Before bills. Before rent. Before groceries. Before anything except God. This is not selfishness. This is stewardship of your future. You are saving for your family's security. You are building wealth that provides options. You are creating margin that prevents emergencies from becoming catastrophes. Saving yourself second is wisdom, not greed.

- Third: Your Future (Reserves and Investments)

After giving and saving, you fund your future. Emergency funds protect you from setbacks. Retirement accounts compound into financial independence. Investment accounts build generational wealth. These allocations are not optional. These allocations are what transform income into lasting wealth. You fund your future before you fund your lifestyle.

- Fourth: Essential Obligations (Housing, Utilities, Transportation, Insurance)

Now you fund survival. Shelter, power, transportation to work, protection through insurance. These expenses keep you alive and employed. These expenses are non-negotiable. But they come fourth, not first. You honored God. You saved. You invested. Now you cover essentials.

- Fifth: Variable Necessities (Food, Household Supplies, Basic Personal Care)

After fixed obligations, you fund variable necessities. Groceries, toiletries, basic household supplies. These items are essential but controllable. You need food. You choose how much to spend on food. You need personal care items. You choose whether to buy premium or generic. Variable necessities get funded after fixed essentials.

- Sixth: Debt Elimination

If you carry debt, you attack it aggressively at this level. After essentials and necessities are covered, every extra dollar goes to eliminating debt. Not making minimum payments—those are part of essential obligations. This is extra payment to accelerate elimination. Debt limits your freedom. Debt transfers your wealth to creditors. Eliminate it.

- Seventh: Discretionary Spending (Entertainment, Dining Out, Hobbies, Upgrades)

Only after everything above is funded do you allocate to lifestyle. Entertainment, restaurants, hobbies, conveniences, luxuries—these come last. If you have money left after funding categories one through six, you spend some on lifestyle. If you do not have money left, you do not spend. Discretionary spending is funded with surplus, never with funds needed elsewhere.

This hierarchy is not arbitrary. This hierarchy reflects spiritual priority, economic necessity, and wealth-building logic. Follow this sequence and you will build wealth. Ignore this sequence and you will stay broke no matter how much you earn.

The remainder of this chapter explains how to implement each level of the hierarchy. You will learn specific percentages, practical systems, and proven methods for allocating every dollar according to the Power Budget framework. You will learn how to make allocation automatic so discipline becomes effortless. You will learn how to protect your allocation from the temptations and pressures that destroy most budgets.

Income creates power. Allocation directs that power. Direction determines destination. Your allocation today determines your financial position in five years, ten years, twenty years. Allocate wisely. Build wealth systematically. Honor God. Secure your future. Achieve financial freedom.

Let's begin.

The First Law of Wealth Building: Pay Yourself First

Most people have their financial priorities backwards.

They get paid. They pay their rent. They pay their car. They pay their utilities. They pay their credit cards. They buy groceries. They buy gas. They buy whatever else they think they need. Then, if there is anything left over, they save it.

There is never anything left over.

This is why most people never save money. They are using the wrong system. They are putting savings last. Savings last means savings never.

Here is the right system: Pay yourself first.

When you get paid, the first thing you do is move money to savings. Before rent. Before bills. Before groceries. Before anything.

You get paid. You save. Then you live on what is left.

This is the first law of wealth building. If you violate this law, you will stay broke no matter how much you make.

The Spiritual Principle: First Fruits

The concept of paying yourself first is not modern financial advice. This is ancient biblical wisdom. The principle of first fruits appears throughout Scripture. God commanded Israel to bring Him the first and best of their harvest, not the leftovers.

Proverbs 3:9-10 states: "Honor the Lord with your wealth and with the first fruits of all your produce; then your barns will be filled with plenty, and your vats will be bursting with wine."

First fruits meant bringing God the initial portion of the harvest before you knew what remained. You did not calculate your needs first and give God the surplus. You gave first, trusting that God would provide for your needs from what remained. This required faith. This demonstrated priority. This honored God above personal security.

The same principle applies to savings. Paying yourself first means allocating to your future before you know what remains. You do not pay all your bills, cover all your wants, and save whatever surplus exists. You save first, trusting that you can live on what remains. This requires discipline. This demonstrates priority. This honors your future above present consumption.

God designed the first fruits principle to train His people in trust and priority. When you give first or save first, you declare that God's provision matters more than your fear. You declare that future security matters more than present comfort. You break the pattern of leftovers. You establish a pattern of priority.

Most people give God their leftovers. Most people save their leftovers. They honor everything else first—bills, lifestyle, desires, immediate gratification. Then they give God and their future whatever remains. Usually nothing remains. This pattern keeps you broke spiritually and financially.

Pay yourself first. Honor your future. Trust that you can live on what remains after you save. This is first fruits applied to wealth building. This is biblical stewardship. This is how you multiply your talent.

The Business Logic: Capital Before Operations

Every successful business allocates capital before it allocates operational spending. Businesses set aside reserves first. They fund growth investments first. They protect cash flow first. Then they pay operating expenses from what remains.

Why? Because businesses that fund operations first and save later always run out of money. They spend every dollar on immediate needs. They have nothing left for emergencies, opportunities, or growth. They operate on razor-thin margins with no buffer. One bad month destroys them.

Businesses that allocate capital first survive downturns, seize opportunities, and grow. They have reserves when unexpected expenses hit. They have investment capital when good opportunities appear. They have cash flow margins that provide stability. They prioritize long-term strength over short-term convenience.

You, Inc. must operate the same way. Your savings and investments are your capital allocation. Your expenses are your operational costs. If you fund operations first and save later, you will always run out of money. You will have nothing left for emergencies, opportunities, or wealth building. You will live paycheck to paycheck with no buffer. One bad month will destroy you.

If you allocate capital first—saving before spending—you build reserves, create opportunities, and grow wealth. You have money when emergencies hit. You have capital when opportunities appear. You have margin that provides stability. You prioritize long-term security over short-term consumption.

This is not complicated. This is basic cash-flow management. Every competent CFO understands this. You are the CFO of You, Inc. Understand this. Implement this. Save first. Spend second. Build wealth.

Why Pay Yourself First Works

When you pay bills first and save last, saving is optional. Saving is whatever is left over. Saving is the thing you do if you have extra money.

You never have extra money. There is always something else to buy. There is always another expense. There is always a reason not to save this month.

When you pay yourself first, saving is mandatory. Saving

is not optional. Saving is not whatever is left over. Saving happens before you have a chance to spend the money.

The money moves to savings before you see it. Before you touch it. Before you can spend it.

This is why automatic transfers work. This is why direct deposit to savings works. This is why paying yourself first works.

The money disappears before you can waste it.

The Psychological Advantage: Removing Temptation

Behavioral economics has proven that humans have limited willpower. You intend to save. You plan to save. You want to save. But when you see money in your checking account, you spend it. You see the balance. You feel wealthy. You justify purchases. You tell yourself you will save next month. Next month never comes.

Paying yourself first removes this temptation. The money is gone before temptation arrives. You never see it in your checking account. You never feel wealthy because of it. You never justify spending it. You adjust your lifestyle to match what remains.

This is pre-commitment. You make the decision to save when you are rational and clear-headed. You automate the decision. Then the decision executes automatically every pay period. You remove the daily willpower requirement. You eliminate the opportunity to fail.

People fail at saving not because they lack desire but because they face temptation dozens of times per day. Every purchase is an opportunity to choose spending over saving. If you face this choice forty times per day, you will fail eventually. Willpower is a limited resource. Temptation is unlimited.

Paying yourself first reduces the choice to one moment: the moment you set up automatic transfers. You make the decision once. The system executes forever. You win because you stopped fighting a battle you could not win through willpower alone.

How to Set Up Pay Yourself First

Here is how to implement this system today.

- *Step 1: Calculate 10% of Your Take-Home Pay*

Look at your paycheck. Find your take-home amount—after taxes, after insurance, after retirement deductions. Multiply by 0.10.

Example: Your take-home pay is $3,000 per month.

$3,000 × 0.10 = $300
You will save $300 per month.
If you are paid biweekly, divide your monthly savings by 2.
$300 ÷ 2 = $150 per paycheck

- *Step 2: Open a Separate Savings Account*

Do not save in your checking account. Money in your checking account gets spent. You will see it. You will justify spending it. It will disappear.

Open a separate savings account. A different bank is even better. Make it difficult to access this money. No debit card. No checks. No easy transfers.

The harder it is to access, the less likely you are to raid it for non-emergencies.

Online high-yield savings accounts work well for this purpose. They pay better interest than traditional savings accounts. They take one to three business days to transfer money back to checking. This delay creates friction. Friction prevents impulse spending from savings.

- *Step 3: Set Up Automatic Transfer*

Set up an automatic transfer from your checking account to your savings account. The transfer should happen the same day you get paid or the day after.

If you get paid on the 1st and 15th, set transfers for the 2nd and 16th.

If you get paid every Friday, set the transfer for every Friday.

Automatic. Same day every time. No thinking required. No decisions to make. The money moves before you can stop it.

Most banks allow you to set up automatic transfers through online banking. Log in. Find the transfers section. Set up a recurring transfer. Choose the amount. Choose the frequency. Choose the date. Save. Done.

If your bank does not offer easy automatic transfers, consider switching banks. A bank that makes automation difficult is a bank working against your wealth building.

- *Step 4: Forget the Money Exists*

Once the money goes to savings, forget about it. Do not check the balance every day. Do not calculate what you could buy with it. Do not tell yourself you will borrow from it and pay it back.

That money is gone. That money is not yours to spend. That money is your future self's money.

Your current self pays your future self first. Your current self lives on what is left.

Train yourself to think of your take-home pay as your income minus automatic savings. If you get paid $3,000 and $300 goes to savings automatically, your real available income is $2,700. Build your budget around $2,700. Live on $2,700. Never touch the $300 in savings except for true emergencies or when you deploy it toward wealth-building goals.

This mental adjustment is critical. Most people think of their full paycheck as available money. They budget the full amount. Then they wonder why they never save. You will think differently. You will consider money already gone. You will live on what remains. This is the mindset shift that makes pay-yourself-first work.

What If I Cannot Afford 10%?

Here is what people tell me:

"I cannot afford to save 10%. My bills are too high. My income is too low. I have nothing left over."

My response: You cannot afford not to save 10%.

If you cannot save 10% of your income, you have a crisis. You are living beyond your means. You are spending money you should be saving. You are prioritizing current comfort over future security.

Here is the truth: You can afford 10%. You just have to cut expenses to make room for it.

Go back to your one-month audit from Chapter 2. Look at your low priority expenses. How much did you waste on restaurants, coffee shops, entertainment, subscriptions, impulse purchases?

For most people, that number is $200-$500 per month. Cut that waste. Redirect it to savings. Now you can afford 10%.

"But I need those things to enjoy life."

No you do not. You need savings to survive life. You need an emergency fund so one car repair does not destroy you. You need savings so you can eventually buy a home. You need savings so you can retire with dignity.

Cut the waste. Save the 10%. Non-negotiable.

What If I Already Save Through My 401k?

Here is what people tell me:

"I already save. I put money in my 401k. Isn't that enough?"

No.

Your 401k is retirement savings. You cannot access that money until you are 59½ years old without penalties. That money does not help you when your car breaks down next month. That money does not help you when you lose your job next year. That money does not help you buy a house in three years.

You need accessible savings. You need an emergency fund. You need liquid cash you can use when life happens.

The 10% pay-yourself-first savings is separate from retirement. This is your emergency fund. This is your down payment fund. This is your freedom fund.

Once you have a fully funded emergency fund (we will talk about this later in this chapter), then you can increase your retirement contributions. But not before.

First priority: Emergency fund through pay-yourself-first savings. Second priority: Increase retirement contributions.

Get the order right.

What If I Have Debt?

Here is what people tell me:

"Should I save or should I pay off debt first?"

This is the wrong question. The right question is: "How do I do both?"

You must save and pay off debt at the same time. Here is why:

If you put all your money toward debt and save nothing, you have no emergency fund. When an emergency happens (and emergencies always happen), you go into more debt. You are running on a treadmill. You pay off debt, then you create new debt. You never get ahead.

You need an emergency fund while you are paying off debt. The emergency fund prevents you from creating new debt when life happens.

Here is the strategy:

Save 10% first (pay yourself first). Make minimum payments on all debts. Put any extra money toward your smallest debt (debt snowball method).

Once you have a starter emergency fund ($1,000-$2,000), you can temporarily pause additional savings and attack debt more aggressively. But you must have that starter fund first.

We will talk more about debt elimination in later chapters. For now, understand this: You must save even while you have debt. Both. At the same time.

The Allocation Formula: Where Your Money Should Go

Now that you are paying yourself first with 10% to savings, you need to allocate the remaining 90% of your income.

Most people allocate randomly. They pay whatever bills show up. They spend whatever they feel like spending. They hope it all works out. It never does.

You are going to allocate intentionally. You are going to assign every dollar a job before the month begins. You are going to follow a proven formula that keeps your spending under control.

Here is the allocation formula I recommend:

10% - Savings (automatic, pay yourself first) 25% - Housing 10% - Utilities 10% - Transportation 15% - Food (groceries only) 10% - Emergency Fund (separate from the 10% savings above) 10% - Debt Elimination 10% - Everything Else (personal care, clothing, entertainment, etc.)

Total: 100% of your take-home income.

Let me break down each category and explain why these percentages matter.

10% - Savings (Automatic, Pay Yourself First)

We already covered this. This is the first 10% that comes out before you do anything else.

This money goes to a separate savings account. This money is for long-term goals (down payment on a house, investment opportunities, wealth building).

This is not your emergency fund (that is separate). This is not your vacation fund (vacations are not a priority right now). This is wealth-building savings.

Non-negotiable. First priority. Automatic. Every paycheck.

25% – Housing

Housing is usually your biggest expense. For most people, housing should be 25-30% of take-home income.

Housing includes:

- Rent or mortgage payment
- Property taxes (if you own)
- Homeowners insurance or renters insurance
- HOA fees (if applicable)
- Basic home maintenance (small repairs, minor upkeep)

If your housing is more than 30% of income, you have a problem. You are house poor. You are spending too much on shelter and not enough on everything else.

The Spiritual Reality: Shelter Is Provision, Not Identity

God provides shelter as a gift. You need a place to live. Scripture acknowledges this basic need. But Scripture also warns against seeking security in houses rather than in God.

Proverbs 24:27 instructs: "Prepare your work outside; get everything ready for yourself in the field, and after that build your house." First establish your economic foundation. Then build your dwelling. Do not invert this order. Do not build beyond your means and then struggle to sustain it.

Jesus taught His disciples not to worry about where they would live or what they would wear. Matthew 6:31-33 states: "Therefore do not be anxious, saying, 'What shall we eat?' or 'What shall we drink?' or 'What shall we wear?' For the Gentiles seek after all these things, and your heavenly Father knows that you need them all. But seek first the kingdom of God and his righteousness, and all these things will be added to you."

Your house is shelter, not identity. Your house is provision, not status. Your house should serve your mission, not define your worth. When you spend 40-50% of your income on housing to impress others or to feel successful, you violate this principle. You seek identity in your house rather than in God. You sacrifice your financial future for a temporary feeling of accomplishment.

God cares that you have shelter. God does not care if your shelter impresses your neighbors. Spend what you need for safe, functional housing. Do not spend what you want to project an image of success. The image is false. The financial damage is real.

The Business Reality: Fixed Costs Determine Survival

In business, fixed costs are the expenses you must pay regardless of revenue. Rent for your office. Lease payments on equipment. Salaries for core staff. These costs do not fluctuate month to month. You owe them whether you make sales or not.

Businesses with high fixed costs operate on thin margins. If revenue drops, they cannot cut fixed costs quickly enough. They go bankrupt. Businesses with low fixed costs survive downturns. If revenue drops, they cut variable costs and survive on lower margins until revenue recovers. They endure.

Your housing is your largest fixed cost. This cost does not change based on your income fluctuations. If you lose hours at work, your rent stays the same. If you lose your job, your mortgage stays the same. If the economy crashes, your housing payment stays the same.

High housing costs create fragility. You are one income disruption away from disaster. If your housing is 40% of your income, you have 60% remaining for everything else. Lose 20% of your income and you are in crisis. You cannot cut housing expenses quickly. You have a lease. You have a mortgage. You are locked in. You collapse financially.

Low housing costs create resilience. If your housing is 25% of your income, you have 75% remaining for everything else. Lose 20% of your income and you still survive. You cut variable expenses. You reduce discretionary spending. You tighten your budget. But you survive. You recover. You avoid catastrophe.

This is not theory. This is what happened to millions of Americans in 2008-2009. People who bought too much house lost everything when income dropped or jobs disappeared. They could not cut housing costs fast enough. They foreclosed. People who bought appropriate housing survived. They cut other expenses. They adjusted. They kept their homes. Housing costs determined who survived and who collapsed.

Keep your housing costs low. Protect yourself from future income shocks. Build resilience into You, Inc. by maintaining low fixed costs. This is basic business survival logic applied to personal finance.

The Behavioral Reality: Lifestyle Inflation Starts with Housing

Lifestyle inflation is the pattern of increasing spending as income increases. You get a raise. You spend more. You get another raise. You spend even more. Your income increases thirty percent over five years. Your spending increases thirty percent. You save nothing additional. You build no additional wealth. The raise changed nothing financially.

Housing is where lifestyle inflation often begins. You make $40,000. You rent a modest apartment for $800. You get a raise. You now make $50,000. You move to a nicer apartment for $1,200. You got a 25% raise. Your rent increased 50%. Your net financial position actually worsened despite the raise.

Three years later, you make $60,000. You buy a house with a $1,600 mortgage payment. Your income increased 50% from your starting point. Your housing costs doubled. You feel successful because you own a home. You are actually more financially fragile than when you made $40,000. Your fixed costs consumed your raises. You cannot save more. You cannot invest more. You just have a nicer address.

This pattern destroys wealth building. Income growth should increase your savings rate, not your lifestyle costs. If you make $40,000 and save 10%, you save $4,000 annually. If you make $60,000 and still save 10%, you save $6,000 annually. This is good. But if you make $60,000 and increase housing costs dramatically, you might only save 5% now. You save $3,000 annually. You make 50% more income. You save 25% less money. This is lifestyle inflation. This is backwards wealth building.

Keep housing costs fixed as income grows. Do not

upgrade your house every time you get a raise. Live in the modest apartment longer. Live in the smaller house longer. Save the income growth. Invest the income growth. Build wealth with the income growth. Let your net worth increase while your housing costs stay stable. This is how you actually benefit from raises and promotions.

The temptation to upgrade housing is powerful. Your friends buy bigger houses. Your family comments on your modest living situation. You feel like you should own something nicer. You see beautiful homes online and imagine living there. Resist these temptations. They lead to financial bondage, not financial freedom. Choose wealth over appearance. Choose options over comfort. Choose a smaller house and a larger savings account.

What if Your Housing Costs Are Too High?

Here is what people tell me:

"But housing is expensive where I live. I cannot find anything cheaper."
Yes you can. You can find a cheaper apartment. You can get a roommate. You can move to a less expensive neighborhood. You can move to a less expensive city.
"But I do not want to do those things."
Then you do not want to build wealth. You want to stay comfortable and stay broke.
Housing is not negotiable in the sense that you need shelter. But the amount you spend on housing is 100% negotiable. You choose where you live. You choose how much you pay.

If your housing is more than 30% of income, you have three options:

1. Increase your income so the percentage drops.

2. Move to cheaper housing.
3. Stay broke.

Pick option 1 or 2. Option 3 is not acceptable.

10% - Utilities

Utilities include:

- Electric
- Gas
- Water
- Sewer
- Trash
- Internet
- Phone (cell phone, landline if you still have one)

Utilities should be 5-10% of income. If your utilities are more than 10%, you are using too much or paying too much.

Ways to reduce utility costs:

Electric and Gas:

- Turn off lights when you leave rooms
- Unplug devices when not in use
- Use a programmable thermostat
- Set temperature higher in summer, lower in winter
- Use fans instead of AC when possible
- Wash clothes in cold water
- Air dry clothes instead of using the dryer
- Replace old appliances with energy-efficient models

Water:

- Take shorter showers
- Fix leaks immediately
- Do not leave water running while brushing teeth or washing dishes
- Use low-flow shower heads and faucets
- Run dishwasher and washing machine only when full

Internet:

- Call your provider and negotiate a lower rate
- Switch to a cheaper plan with lower speeds (most people do not need the fastest internet)
- Bundle services if it saves money
- Consider switching providers for new customer discounts

Phone:

- Switch to a cheaper carrier (Mint Mobile, Cricket, Metro by T-Mobile, etc.)
- Reduce your data plan (most people do not need unlimited data)
- Remove insurance and protection plans (these are usually not worth it)
- Stop financing phones (buy phones outright or use older models)

Most people can cut their utility costs by 20-40% with these strategies. That is $50-$100 per month. That is $600-$1,200 per year.

Do the work. Make the cuts. Redirect the savings to your emergency fund or debt elimination.

10% - Transportation

Transportation includes:

- Car payment (if you have one)
- Car insurance
- Gas
- Maintenance (oil changes, tire rotations, repairs)
- Registration and tags
- Parking fees
- Tolls
- Public transportation

Transportation should be 10-15% of income. If your transportation is more than 15%, you are spending too much on your car.

The biggest problem in this category is car payments. Car payments destroy budgets. Car payments keep people broke.

Here is the truth: You cannot afford a car payment.

"But I need a car to get to work."

Yes. You need a car. You do not need a new car. You do not need a $400 car payment. You do not need a luxury vehicle.

You need reliable transportation. You can get reliable transportation for $3,000-$8,000 cash.

"But I do not have $3,000-$8,000 cash."

Then sell your current car (yes, even if you are upside down), use whatever money you get, save the rest, and buy a cheap car cash.

"But if I sell my car, I will owe money."

So what? Pay off the difference over time while you drive a cheap car you own. That is still better than having a car payment forever.

Here is the math:

Scenario 1: Keep your car with payments

- Car payment: $400/month
- Insurance on newer car: $150/month
- Total: $550/month
- Annual cost: $6,600

Scenario 2: Sell your car, buy a cheap car cash

- Car payment: $0
- Insurance on older car: $80/month
- Maintenance fund: $100/month (you will need repairs on an older car)
- Total: $180/month
- Annual cost: $2,160
- Annual savings: $4,440

You save $4,440 per year by driving a cheap car you own. That is your emergency fund. That is your down payment. That is your debt elimination money. That is your wealth building.

But you have to be willing to drive an ugly car for a few years. You have to be willing to give up the new car smell. You have to be willing to let go of your ego.

Most people will not do this. Most people need a nice car to feel successful. Those people stay broke while looking successful.

You are not most people. You are willing to do what most people will not do so you can have what most people will never have.

Sell the car. Buy a beater. Save the difference. Build wealth.

15% - Food (Groceries Only)

Food should be 10-15% of income. This is groceries only. Eating out comes from a different category (the 10% "everything else" category).

RUN YOUR HOUSEHOLD LIKE A BUSINESS

Most people spend too much on food. They buy name brands when generics cost half as much. They buy prepared foods when cooking from scratch costs less. They waste food because they do not plan meals. They let produce rot because they forgot they bought it.

Here is how to reduce your grocery bill:

Plan Your Meals

- Plan every meal for the week before you shop
- Make a grocery list based on your meal plan
- Buy only what is on the list
- Do not shop when hungry (you will buy more)

Buy Generic

- Store brands cost 20-40% less than name brands
- Most generic products are identical to name brands (same manufacturer, different label)
- Try generic for everything. If you do not like something, switch back to name brand for that item only

Cook from Scratch

- Pre-made meals cost 2-3 times more than cooking from ingredients
- Buy whole chickens and cut them up yourself (cheaper than buying parts)
- Make your own snacks instead of buying packaged snacks
- Bake your own bread (costs pennies per loaf)

Buy in Bulk

- Rice, beans, pasta, oats, flour, sugar all store well and cost less in bulk
- Freeze meat when you find sales
- Stock up on non-perishables when they are on sale

Reduce Meat

- Meat is expensive
- Eat more beans, lentils, eggs (cheap protein)
- Use meat as a flavoring instead of the main dish
- Have meatless meals 2-3 times per week

Stop Wasting Food

- Use leftovers for lunch the next day
- Freeze leftovers if you cannot eat them within 2-3 days
- Use vegetable scraps to make stock
- Check your refrigerator before shopping so you do not buy duplicates

Shop Sales and Use Coupons

- Check the weekly ad before shopping
- Plan meals around what is on sale
- Use coupons for items you already buy (do not buy something just because you have a coupon)
- Use cashback apps (Ibotta, Fetch, Checkout 51)

Most people can cut their grocery bill by 30-50% with these strategies. A family spending $800 on groceries can cut that to $400-$500.

That is $300-$400 per month saved. That is $3,600-$4,800 per year. That is wealth-building money.

Do the work. Plan your meals. Cook from scratch. Stop wasting food.

10% - Emergency Fund

This is separate from your 10% pay-yourself-first savings.

The pay-yourself-first savings is for long-term wealth building. The emergency fund is for emergencies.

What is an emergency?

- Your car breaks down and you need repairs to get to work
- You lose your job and need to pay bills while you find a new one
- You have a medical emergency and need to pay the deductible
- Your refrigerator dies and you need to replace it
- Your roof starts leaking and needs immediate repair

What is NOT an emergency?

- Christmas (you know it is coming every year)
- Birthdays (you know when your birthday is)
- Vacations (vacations are planned, not emergencies)
- New clothes (you do not need new clothes)
- Wanting to eat out (that is not an emergency)
- Sale at your favorite store (a sale is not an emergency)

Most people use their emergency fund for non-emergencies. Then when a real emergency happens, they have no money and they go into debt.

Do not do this. The emergency fund is sacred. The emergency fund is only for real emergencies.

How much should you have in your emergency fund?

Starter Emergency Fund: $1,000-$2,000

This is your first goal. Save $1,000-$2,000 as fast as possible. This covers most small emergencies (car repairs, minor medical bills, small home repairs).

Once you have your starter emergency fund, you can focus on debt elimination while continuing to build your full emergency fund.

Full Emergency Fund: 6-12 Months of Expenses

This is your ultimate goal. Save enough to cover 6-12 months of living expenses.

Why 6-12 months? Because that is how long it might take you to find a new job if you lose your current job. That is how long you need to survive without income.

Calculate your monthly essential expenses (rent, utilities, food, insurance, minimum debt payments). Multiply by 6 or 12.
Example: Monthly essential expenses: $2,500 6 months: $2,500 × 6 = $15,000 12 months: $2,500 × 12 = $30,000
Your full emergency fund should be $15,000-$30,000.

This sounds impossible. It is not. It just takes time and discipline.

If you save 10% of your income toward emergency fund every month:

- Income: $4,000/month
- 10% to emergency fund: $400/month

- Time to save $15,000: $15,000 ÷ $400 = 37.5 months (about 3 years)

Three years sounds like a long time. But three years will pass whether you save or not. In three years, you can have a fully funded emergency fund and total peace of mind, or you can still be living paycheck to paycheck with no security.

Choose peace of mind. Start saving today.

Where to Keep Your Emergency Fund

Do not keep your emergency fund in your checking account. You will spend it.

Do not keep your emergency fund in cash at home. You might spend it. Someone might steal it. You might lose it in a fire or flood.

Keep your emergency fund in a savings account. A high-yield savings account is even better (these pay more interest).

Some people use money market accounts. Some people use short-term CDs. Some people split their emergency fund between multiple accounts.

The key is this: The money should be accessible within 1-3 days, but not so accessible that you spend it on non-emergencies.

No debit card for this account. No checks. Transfer money only when you have a real emergency.

10% - Debt Elimination

If you have debt (credit cards, student loans, personal loans, medical debt, car loans), allocate 10% of your income to debt elimination.

This is on top of your minimum payments. Your minimum payments are already included in your budget (credit cards might be in the "everything else" category, car loan is in transportation, etc.).

This 10% is extra money that goes toward eliminating debt faster.

Here is the strategy (this is called the debt snowball method):

Step 1: List all your debts from smallest to largest balance

Ignore interest rates. Focus on balance only.
Example:

- Credit Card 1: $500
- Medical Bill: $800
- Credit Card 2: $2,000
- Car Loan: $8,000
- Student Loan: $25,000

Step 2: Make minimum payments on everything

You must make minimum payments on all debts to avoid late fees and damage to your credit score.

Step 3: Put all your extra money (the 10% allocation) toward the smallest debt

In the example above, you would put all your extra money toward Credit Card 1 ($500 balance).

Step 4: When the smallest debt is paid off, celebrate

You eliminated a debt. You accomplished something. Celebrate for one day. Then get back to work.

Step 5: Take the payment you were making on the smallest debt and add it to the payment on the next smallest debt

In the example above, once Credit Card 1 is paid off, you take that payment plus your extra 10% and apply it all to the Medical Bill ($800).

This is the snowball. Each time you pay off a debt, the payment gets bigger for the next debt. The snowball rolls faster and faster.

Step 6: Repeat until all debts are paid off

This method works because of psychology. When you pay off small debts quickly, you see progress. When you see progress, you stay motivated. When you stay motivated, you keep going.

Some people argue you should pay off high-interest debt first. Mathematically, they are right. You will save more money on interest that way.

But personal finance is more personal than finance. Motivation matters more than math. Quick wins matter more than optimal interest savings.

Pay off the smallest debts first. Build momentum. Stay motivated. Eliminate all your debt.

How Long Does Debt Elimination Take?

This depends on how much debt you have and how much extra money you can put toward it.

Let me give you some examples:

Example 1: $10,000 in debt, $400/month toward debt elimination

- Time to pay off: $10,000 ÷ $400 = 25 months (about 2 years)
- Example 2: $30,000 in debt, $600/month toward debt elimination

- Time to pay off: $30,000 ÷ $600 = 50 months (about 4 years)
- Example 3: $50,000 in debt, $800/month toward debt elimination
- Time to pay off: $50,000 ÷ $800 = 62.5 months (about 5 years)

These are approximate calculations that do not account for interest, but they give you an idea of timeline.

Four or five years sounds like a long time. But four or five years will pass whether you eliminate your debt or not. In five years, you can be debt-free, or you can still be making minimum payments and getting nowhere.

Choose debt-free. Start today.

What if I Do Not Have Any Debt?

Congratulations. You are ahead of most people.

If you have no debt, redirect the 10% debt elimination allocation to your emergency fund. Get to a full 6-12 month emergency fund faster.

Once your emergency fund is fully funded, redirect the money to your long-term savings and investments. Increase your retirement contributions. Save for a house down payment. Build wealth.

10% - Everything Else

This is the category for everything that does not fit above:

- Eating out (restaurants, coffee shops, fast food, delivery)
- Personal care (haircuts, grooming, gym membership)

- Clothing (clothes, shoes, accessories)
- Entertainment (movies, concerts, streaming services, cable, hobbies)
- Gifts (birthdays, holidays, weddings, baby showers)
- Charitable giving
- Pet care
- Kids' activities
- Miscellaneous expenses

Ten percent might sound low. It is supposed to be low. This category is luxuries. Luxuries get the smallest allocation.

Most people spend 30-40% of their income in this category. Then they wonder why they have no savings.

You are going to spend 10%. You are going to prioritize wealth building over current comfort. You are going to delay gratification so you can have freedom later.

Here is how to make 10% work:

Eating Out: Reduce by 80-90%

If you currently spend $400 on eating out, cut it to $40-$80. Pack lunches. Cook at home. Make coffee at home. Stop using food delivery apps.

Eating out is not a necessity. Eating out is a luxury. Treat it like a luxury. Once per month. Special occasions only.

Personal Care: Reduce by 50%

Get haircuts less frequently. Skip the salon and go to a barber or budget hair place. Do your own nails. Cancel your gym membership (exercise at home or outside).

You do not need to spend $200 per month on personal care. You need to be clean and presentable. That costs $40-$50 per month, not $200.

Clothing: Reduce by 70-80%

Stop buying new clothes every month. You do not need more clothes. You need to save money.

Buy clothes when your current clothes are worn out. Shop thrift stores. Shop clearance racks. Buy off-season (buy winter clothes in summer, summer clothes in winter).

Most people can go 3-6 months without buying any clothes. Try it.

Entertainment: Reduce by 80-90%

Cancel cable. Keep one streaming service (not five). Use the library (free books, movies, music). Do free activities (hiking, parks, free community events).

Entertainment should cost less than $50 per month. Most people spend $150-$300. Cut it.

Gifts: Plan Ahead

Set a monthly budget for gifts ($20-$40). Save it every month. When birthdays and holidays come, you have money set aside.

Do not go into debt for gifts. Do not use credit cards for gifts. Give what you can afford within your budget.

Make gifts instead of buying them (baked goods, photo albums, handmade items). Give experiences instead of things (time together, home-cooked meals). Give less expensive gifts.

Nobody needs you to go into debt to buy them gifts. If they expect that, they do not care about you. They care about what they can get from you.

Bottom Line

The "everything else" category is where you prove your

commitment to change. This is where discipline shows up. This is where you choose your future over your present.

Most people cannot do this. Most people need their luxuries. Most people need to eat out and buy new clothes and have all the streaming services.

Those people stay broke.

You are not most people. You will make the cuts. You will live on 10% for everything else. You will build wealth while everyone else builds debt.

The 20% Savings Rule

Let me add everything up:

- 10% - Pay yourself first (automatic savings)
- 10% - Emergency fund

That is 20% of your income going to savings.

This is the minimum. This is what you must save to build wealth. If you are not saving 20% of your income, you are not building wealth. You are maintaining your current situation at best. More likely, you are slowly going broke.

"But I cannot save 20%. That is too much."

No. You cannot afford not to save 20%.

Let me show you what happens when you save 20% vs. when you save nothing:

Person A: Saves 20% ($800/month on $4,000 income)

- After 1 year: $9,600 saved
- After 5 years: $48,000 saved (plus interest)
- After 10 years: $96,000 saved (plus interest)
- After 20 years: $192,000 saved (plus interest)

Person B: Saves nothing

- After 1 year: $0
- After 5 years: $0
- After 10 years: $0
- After 20 years: $0

Person A can buy a house. Person B cannot. Person A can survive losing a job. Person B cannot. Person A can retire. Person B cannot.

Person A has options. Person B has stress.

Which person do you want to be?

Save 20%. Non-negotiable. Make it happen.

What If My Numbers Do Not Match the Formula?

You did your one-month audit. You calculated your percentages. Your housing is 35%. Your food is 20%. Your transportation is 18%.

Your numbers do not match the formula. Now what?

Now you make changes. You adjust your spending to match the formula. You cut expenses until the numbers work.

"But I cannot cut my rent. I have a lease."

Fine. Your rent is fixed for now. When your lease ends, move to cheaper housing. In the meantime, cut everything else more aggressively to make room for the high rent.

"But I cannot cut my car payment. I have a loan."

Fine. Your car payment is fixed for now. But you can sell the car, pay off the loan (even if you have to add money), and buy a cheap car cash. Or you can ride out the loan and then never have a car payment again. Your choice.

The formula is the target. You might not hit the target immediately. But you work toward it. You make cuts every month. You find ways to reduce expenses. You adjust your lifestyle.

Within 3-6 months, your numbers should be close to the formula. Within 12 months, your numbers should match the formula.

If your numbers are not moving toward the formula, you are not serious about change. You are making excuses. You are choosing comfort over wealth.

Make the cuts. Hit the target. Build wealth.

The Cash Envelope Method for Variable Expenses

You have allocated your money. You know how much goes to each category. Now you need a system to make sure you actually stick to the allocations.

This is where most budgets fail. People know they should only spend $300 on groceries. Then they spend $450 because they do not have a system to stop themselves.

The cash envelope method is that system.

Here is how it works:

Step 1: Identify Your Variable Expense Categories

Variable expenses are expenses that change every month based on your choices.

Fixed expenses are expenses that stay the same every month (rent, car payment, insurance).

Variable expenses include:

- Groceries
- Gas
- Eating out (restaurants, coffee, fast food)
- Entertainment
- Personal care

- Clothing
- Miscellaneous

Step 2: Determine Your Budget for Each Category

Based on the allocation formula, calculate how much you will spend in each variable expense category.

Example (based on $4,000 monthly income):

- Groceries: $600 (15% of income)
- Gas: $200 (5% of income, part of transportation)
- Eating out: $80 (2% of income, part of everything else)
- Personal care: $40 (1% of income, part of everything else)
- Entertainment: $40 (1% of income, part of everything else)
- Clothing: $40 (1% of income, part of everything else)

Step 3: Get Cash and Create Envelopes

Go to the bank. Withdraw cash for all your variable expense categories.

Get envelopes (you can buy them or use regular envelopes you already have). Label each envelope with the category name and the amount.

Envelope 1: Groceries - $600 Envelope 2: Gas - $200 Envelope 3: Eating Out - $80 Envelope 4: Personal Care - $40 Envelope 5: Entertainment - $40 Envelope 6: Clothing - $40

Put the cash in each envelope.

Step 4: Spend Only What Is in the Envelope

When you need to buy groceries, take the grocery envelope. When the envelope is empty, you are done buying groceries for the month.

When you need gas, take the gas envelope. When the envelope is empty, you are done buying gas for the month (use public transportation, carpool, walk, or do not go anywhere unnecessary).

When you want to eat out, take the eating out envelope. When the envelope is empty, you are done eating out for the month. Pack a lunch. Cook at home. No exceptions.

The envelope system works because cash is tangible. When you hand over cash, you feel it. When you see the envelope getting empty, you slow down. When the envelope is empty, you stop.

Credit cards and debit cards do not have this effect. You swipe and swipe and swipe. You do not see the money leaving. You do not feel the pain of spending. You overspend without realizing it.

Cash makes you conscious. Cash makes you think before you spend. Cash keeps you on budget.

Step 5: Do Not Borrow from Other Envelopes

This is the rule people break most often.

The grocery envelope is empty but you need milk. So you take $10 from the gas envelope. No big deal, right?

Wrong. That is the beginning of the end. Once you start borrowing from envelopes, the whole system falls apart.

If the grocery envelope is empty, you are done buying groceries. You eat what you have at home. You get creative with leftovers. You meal plan better next month so this does not happen again.

If you absolutely must have something (milk for your

baby, for example), then you must cut something else. Maybe you skip eating out this month to free up $10 for groceries. But you do not borrow. You make a trade.

No borrowing between envelopes. This rule is non-negotiable.

What About Online Purchases?

The envelope system works best for in-person purchases. But many expenses are paid online (utilities, subscriptions, online shopping).

For online purchases, you have two options:

- Option 1: Pay online with your debit card, then remove the equivalent cash from the envelope

If you buy something online for $40 and it falls under the "clothing" category, pay for it online, then take $40 out of your clothing envelope and put it back in the bank.

This keeps your envelopes accurate. You still see the cash leaving. You still feel the spending.

- Option 2: Do not shop online

The simpler solution is to stop shopping online. Buy only what you can buy in person with cash.

This eliminates impulse purchases. This eliminates browsing online stores. This eliminates one-click buying. This keeps your spending under control.

Most people will not do this. Most people need the convenience of online shopping. Those people will overspend.

You are not most people. Cut the online shopping. Buy only what you need. Use cash only.

What to Do with Money Left Over

At the end of the month, you might have money left in your envelopes.

You budgeted $600 for groceries but only spent $550. You have $50 left over.

You budgeted $200 for gas but only spent $180. You have $20 left over.

You have $70 total left over. What do you do with it?

You have three options:

- Option 1: Roll it over to next month's envelopes

Add the leftover grocery money to next month's grocery envelope. Add the leftover gas money to next month's gas envelope.

This gives you a cushion for months when you need a little extra.

- Option 2: Move it to your emergency fund

Take all leftover money and add it to your emergency fund.

This accelerates your emergency fund. This gets you to full funding faster.

- Option 3: Put it toward debt

Take all leftover money and make an extra payment on your smallest debt.

This accelerates debt elimination. This gets you debt-free faster.

I recommend option 2 or 3. Do not make your envelopes bigger every month. That defeats the purpose of the budget. You are training yourself to live on less, not finding ways to spend more.

Take the leftover money and either save it or pay off debt with it. Build wealth with money you did not spend.

Creating a Zero-Based Budget

The allocation formula gives you percentages. The cash envelope method gives you a spending system. Now you need to put it all together into a zero-based budget.

A zero-based budget means every dollar is assigned a job before the month begins. Income minus expenses equals zero.

Not negative (that means you are spending more than you make). Not positive (that means you have unallocated money that will probably get wasted). Zero.

Every dollar is allocated. Every dollar has a purpose. Nothing is left to chance.

Here is how to create a zero-based budget:

Step 1: Write Down Your Income

Write down your take-home income for the month. This is the money that actually hits your bank account, not your gross salary.

If you get paid biweekly, multiply your paycheck by 2.17 to get your average monthly income (26 paychecks per year ÷ 12 months = 2.17).

If your income varies (commission, tips, freelance, hourly with changing hours), use your lowest monthly income from the past 6 months. Budget conservatively. If you make more, great. Use the extra for savings or debt. Do not budget based on your highest income and then fall short.

Step 2: List All Your Expenses

List every single expense you have. Fixed and variable. Essential and non-essential. Everything.

Use your one-month audit from Chapter 2. Those are your real expenses.

Step 3: Allocate Every Dollar

Start at the top of your expense list. Assign money to each category based on the allocation formula.

10% to automatic savings (pay yourself first) Then allocate the remaining 90%: 25% to housing 10% to utilities 10% to transportation 15% to food (groceries only) 10% to emergency fund 10% to debt elimination 10% to everything else

Write down the dollar amount for each category based on your income.

Step 4: Adjust Until You Hit Zero

Add up all your allocations. Subtract from your income.

If the result is positive, you have unallocated money. Allocate it to savings, emergency fund, or debt elimination. Do not leave it unallocated.

If the result is negative, you allocated more than you make. Cut expenses until you hit zero. This usually means cutting the "everything else" category more aggressively.

Keep adjusting until income minus expenses equals zero.

Step 5: Write It Down

Do not keep your budget in your head. Do not use a mental budget. Write it down.

Use a spreadsheet. Use a budget app. Use pen and paper. Use whatever works for you.

But write it down. A budget in your head is not a budget. A budget in your head is a wish.

Step 6: Review Your Budget with Your Accountability Partner

Before the month begins, meet with your accountability partner. Show them your budget. Let them review it. Let them ask questions. Let them challenge your allocations.

"You allocated $200 for eating out. That is 5% of your income. The formula says 2%. Why are you overspending on eating out?"

Let them hold you accountable. That is why they exist.

Step 7: Track Your Spending Throughout the Month

A budget is a plan. Tracking is execution.

You can have a perfect plan. If you do not execute, the plan is worthless.

Use your cash envelopes for variable expenses. Track your fixed expenses to make sure they match your budget. Check your bank account weekly. Review your spending every Sunday.

Do not wait until the end of the month to see if you stayed on budget. By then it is too late. Check weekly. Adjust as needed.

Step 8: Review at the End of the Month

On the last day of the month, sit down and review.

Did you stick to your budget? Where did you overspend? Where did you underspend? What surprised you? What do you need to change for next month?

Write down your observations. Learn from the month. Adjust your next budget based on what you learned.

Then meet with your accountability partner. Show them your results. Be honest about what went wrong. Commit to doing better next month.

When Your Income Changes

Your income might change from month to month. You might get overtime some months. You might get a bonus. You might work fewer hours. You might lose hours due to holidays or slow season.

When your income changes, your budget changes. But the percentages stay the same.

If you make $4,000 one month and $5,000 the next month, you do not increase all your spending. You keep your spending the same and put the extra $1,000 toward savings, emergency fund, or debt elimination.

If you make $4,000 one month and $3,000 the next month, you cut your spending to match. This usually means cutting the "everything else" category. Your rent does not change. Your utilities are mostly fixed. You cut the variable expenses.

The allocation formula adapts to your income. The percentages stay the same. The dollar amounts change.

This is why percentage-based budgets work better than fixed-amount budgets. Percentages scale with your income. Fixed amounts do not.

Making the System Work Long-Term

The allocation system works. I have seen it work for thousands of people over 35 years.

But here is the truth: The system only works if you work it.

Most people will read this chapter. Most people will nod their heads. Most people will say "this makes sense." Then most people will change nothing.

They will not set up automatic savings. They will not create cash envelopes. They will not do a zero-based budget. They will not meet with their accountability partner.

They will go back to their old habits. They will keep

spending without thinking. They will keep wondering where their money went.

Then they will say "budgeting does not work."

Budgeting works. They just did not work the budget.

You are not most people.

You are going to do the work. You are going to set up the system. You are going to follow the allocation formula. You are going to use cash envelopes. You are going to create zero-based budgets every month. You are going to meet with your accountability partner.

You are going to make this work because your future depends on it.

Your future home depends on it. Your future freedom from debt depends on it. Your future retirement depends on it. Your future security depends on it.

Do the work. Follow the system. Build wealth.

The Bridge to Protection

You now have an operating system. Every dollar has a job. Your income flows through a strategic allocation hierarchy that honors God first, protects your future second, and sustains your present third. You pay yourself before you pay anyone else. You fund essentials before you fund lifestyle. You build wealth systematically through disciplined allocation.

But allocation alone does not build wealth. You must also protect your allocation from waste.

You allocate $600 to groceries. Then you spend $800 because you did not plan meals, you bought prepared foods, you wasted produce, and you ate out when you got tired of cooking. Your allocation was correct. Your execution failed. You wasted $200 that should have stayed in your budget.

You allocate $200 to transportation. Then you spend $350 because you bought premium gas instead of regular, you paid for unnecessary car washes, you ignored maintenance until something broke, and you drove inefficiently. Your allocation was correct. Your execution failed. You wasted $150 that should have stayed in your budget.

You allocate $50 to entertainment. Then you spend $200 because you kept all your streaming services, you went to movies, you bought books you will not read, and you purchased apps you will not use. Your allocation was correct. Your execution failed. You wasted $150 that should have stayed in your budget.

Allocation assigns purpose. Execution protects that purpose. Between purpose and protection lies the difference between wealth and waste.

This is where most budgets fail. People allocate correctly. They spend incorrectly. They know where money should go. They do not control where money actually goes. They have a plan. They do not follow the plan. Their budget exists on paper but not in reality.

You will not make this mistake. You will protect your allocation through aggressive expense management. You will eliminate waste. You will cut spending that serves no purpose. You will prune your financial life like a gardener prunes a tree—removing everything that drains resources without producing fruit.

Chapter 5 teaches you how to prune. How to identify waste. How to eliminate non-essential spending. How to reduce necessary spending. How to cut without suffering. How to protect your allocation from the thousand small leaks that drain wealth slowly and silently.

Allocation creates the structure. Pruning removes the waste. Together, they build wealth that lasts.

You built the structure in this chapter. You learned where money goes and why. You created your allocation percentages. You set up your systems. You established your zero-based budget. You automated your savings. You prepared your cash envelopes.

Now you protect what you built. Now you eliminate spending that does not serve your mission. Now you cut aggressively so your allocation succeeds.

Turn the page. Learn to prune. Master expense elimination. Complete your wealth-building system.

Your Assignment for This Chapter

Do not move to Chapter 4 until you complete this assignment.

- Step 1: Calculate 10% of your take-home income. This is your pay-yourself-first amount.
- Step 2: Open a separate savings account if you do not already have one.
- Step 3: Set up automatic transfer from checking to savings for 10% of every paycheck. Do this today.
- Step 4: Calculate your allocation amounts for all categories based on the formula (25% housing, 10% utilities, etc.).
- Step 5: Create cash envelopes for all variable expense categories. Withdraw cash. Fill the envelopes.
- Step 6: Create your first zero-based budget. Write it down. Make sure income minus expenses equals zero.
- Step 7: Review your budget with your accountability partner before the month begins.
- Step 8: Track your spending all month using your cash envelopes and bank account.
- Step 9: Review your results at the end of the month. Learn from what went wrong. Adjust for next month.

- Step 10: Commit to following this system every month for at least six months. Do not quit after one month. Do not quit after three months. Give the system time to work.

One of the most common mistakes people make is trying to cut expenses before they have an allocation system. That approach almost always fails.

Why? Because without allocation, cutting feels like punishment. With allocation, cutting feels strategic.

Allocation answers the question, "Where should my money go?"

Elimination answers the question, "What is getting in the way?"

You cannot remove obstacles until you know the destination. That is why this chapter comes before Chapter 5. Order matters.

CHAPTER 5
CUTTING EXPENSES – THE ELIMINATION LIST

The Spiritual Foundation: Why God Cares How You Spend

Before we discuss what to cut and how to cut it, you need to understand the theological reality of your spending decisions. This is not just about money. This is about stewardship. This is about faithfulness. This is about whether you multiply your talent or bury it.

Every dollar you waste is a talent buried. Every unnecessary expense is a resource squandered. Every impulse purchase is a choice to serve immediate desire over long-term purpose. God cares about these decisions because God cares about stewardship. You are not spending your money. You are managing God's resources.

The Biblical Mandate: Use Wisely, Waste Nothing

Scripture is clear about waste. After Jesus fed five thousand people with five loaves and two fish, He gave specific instructions about the leftovers. John 6:12 records: "When they had all had enough to eat, he said to his disciples, 'Gather the pieces that are left over. Let nothing be wasted.'"

Let nothing be wasted.

Jesus performed a miracle. Food appeared from nothing. Abundance flowed from scarcity. Yet even in miraculous provision, the command was clear: gather what remains. Use everything. Waste nothing.

If Jesus, who could create food from thin air, commanded His disciples to collect leftovers so nothing would be wasted, how much more should you avoid wasting the resources you work for? You cannot create money miraculously. You trade hours of your life for dollars. Every wasted dollar is wasted life.

Proverbs 21:20 states: "The wise store up choice food and olive oil, but fools gulp theirs down." Wise people save. Wise people preserve resources. Wise people live below their means and build reserves. Fools consume everything immediately. Fools waste resources on temporary pleasure. Fools stay broke because they refuse to exercise restraint.

This is not about legalism. This is about wisdom. God designed a world where waste leads to poverty and stewardship leads to abundance. This is built into creation. This is economic law functioning as spiritual law. You cannot violate these principles without consequences.

Frugality Is Not Poverty—It Is Wisdom

Many people confuse frugality with poverty. They see cutting expenses as deprivation. They resist frugality because they think it makes them look poor. This thinking is backwards and spiritually dangerous.

Frugality is choosing to spend less than you can afford so you can save and invest the difference. Poverty is having no choice. Frugality is power. Poverty is powerlessness.

Frugality is voluntary simplicity that builds wealth. Poverty is involuntary scarcity that perpetuates itself.

Proverbs 13:7 teaches: "One person pretends to be rich, yet has nothing; another pretends to be poor, yet has great wealth." The person pretending to be rich spends everything to look successful. They drive expensive cars they cannot afford. They live in houses that consume all their income. They wear expensive clothes while drowning in debt. They look rich. They are broke.

The person pretending to be poor lives modestly. They drive old cars. They live in modest homes. They buy generic brands. They look ordinary. They are wealthy. They have savings. They have investments. They have options. They have freedom.

Frugality is wisdom. Frugality is choosing long-term abundance over short-term appearance. Frugality is stewarding resources well so you can be generous later, retire comfortably, and leave an inheritance. Frugality honors God because frugality says "I will not waste what You provided."

The Sin of Waste: Using More Than You Need While Others Have Less

Here is a truth most people do not want to hear: waste is sin. Not the worst sin. Not unforgivable sin. But sin nonetheless.

When you waste money on things you do not need while others lack things they desperately need, you are hoarding resources God intended to flow. When you spend four hundred dollars per month eating at restaurants while people in your community cannot afford groceries, that is a stewardship failure. When you pay for five streaming services you barely watch while missionaries struggle to fund their work, that is misaligned priorities. When you buy new clothes every month while your emergency fund sits empty, you are choosing consumption over wisdom.

James 4:17 declares: "If anyone, then, knows the good they ought to do and doesn't do it, it is sin for them." You know you should save. You know you should eliminate debt. You know you should build an emergency fund. You know you should be generous with those in need. When you waste money instead of doing these things, you are sinning through neglect.

This is not condemnation. This is conviction. Conviction produces change. Condemnation produces despair. God convicts you because He loves you. God shows you waste so you can eliminate it. God reveals poor stewardship so you can practice good stewardship.

The purpose of cutting expenses is not just to balance your budget. The purpose is to align your spending with your calling. The purpose is to stop wasting God's provision. The purpose is to steward resources well so you can fulfill your mission, serve your family, bless your community, and advance the Kingdom.

Every Dollar Is a Stewardship Decision

When you spend money, you are making a stewardship decision. You are deciding whether this expense serves your God-given purpose or distracts from it. You are deciding whether this purchase multiplies your talent or buries it. You are deciding whether this spending honors God or serves your flesh.

Most people make these decisions emotionally. They see something they want. They feel desire. They buy. No thought. No prayer. No consideration of stewardship. Just emotion and consumption.

You will make these decisions differently. You will filter every expense through your mission. You will ask: does this spending serve the purpose God gave me? Does this expense help me provide for my family, build wealth, achieve financial freedom, and increase my capacity to serve? If yes, spend. If no, do not spend.

This is not complicated. This is not legalistic. This is stewardship. You are the manager of God's resources. Managers who waste resources get fired. Managers who steward resources well get promoted. You want promotion, not termination.

Cutting Is Not Deprivation—It Is Alignment

The rest of this chapter will show you exactly what to cut and how to cut it. You will eliminate hundreds or thousands of dollars in monthly waste. This will feel uncomfortable initially. Your flesh will resist. Your pride will protest. You will be tempted to make excuses.

Remember this: cutting expenses is not deprivation. Cutting expenses is alignment. You are aligning your spending with your values. You are aligning your budget with your mission. You are aligning your stewardship with God's principles.

When you cut restaurant spending, you are not being deprived of good food. You are choosing to allocate that money to emergency savings instead. When you cut subscription services, you are not being deprived of entertainment. You are choosing to allocate that money to debt elimination instead. When you cut impulse purchases, you are not being deprived of pleasure. You are choosing to allocate that money to wealth building instead.

Every cut creates room for something better. Every elimination funds something more important. Every sacrifice now produces freedom later. This is not deprivation. This is wisdom. This is stewardship. This is faithfulness with little so God can entrust you with much.

Luke 16:10-11 teaches: "Whoever can be trusted with very little can also be trusted with much, and whoever is dishonest with very little will also be dishonest with much. So if you have not been trustworthy in handling worldly wealth, who will trust you with true riches?"

You prove trustworthiness in small things before God trusts you with large things. You prove stewardship with your current income before God increases your capacity. You prove discipline with four hundred dollars per month before God gives you opportunities that generate four thousand per month.

Cutting expenses is the test. Faithful stewardship of limited resources is the proof. God is watching. God is evaluating. God is preparing you for greater responsibility. Pass the test. Cut the waste. Prove faithful with little. Receive much.

Now let's cut.

The Mindset You Need Before You Cut

Before we talk about what to cut, we need to talk about the mindset required to cut successfully.

Cutting expenses hurts. It feels like deprivation. It feels like punishment. It feels like you are taking away everything that makes life enjoyable.

That feeling is temporary. That feeling comes from your brain resisting change. That feeling goes away after thirty to sixty days when your new spending habits become normal.

But most people quit before they get to that point. They cut expenses for two weeks. They feel deprived. They tell themselves this is too hard. They go back to their old spending habits. Then they wonder why they never build wealth.

You cannot quit after two weeks. You cannot quit after one month. You need to commit to at least six months of aggressive expense cutting. Six months. Not six weeks. Six months.

Here is what happens when you commit to six months. Month one hurts. You miss eating out. You miss buying things. You feel restricted. Month two still hurts, but less. You start seeing money accumulate in your savings. That feels good. Month three is easier. Your new habits are forming. You stop thinking about the things you gave up. Month four, you realize you do not miss most of what you cut. Month five, you find new free or cheap activities you enjoy. Month six, the new spending pattern feels normal. You do not feel deprived anymore.

But you have to make it to month six. Most people quit in month one or two.

Here is the second mindset shift you need: This is temporary. You are not cutting expenses forever. You are cutting expenses until you hit your financial goals. Once you have a fully funded emergency fund, once your debt is eliminated, once you have your down payment saved, you can add some expenses back if you want.

But not all of them. Because by month six, you will realize you do not need most of what you cut. You will realize you were wasting money on things that added no real value to your life. You will choose to keep living lean because living lean is what built your wealth.

Here is the third mindset shift: Distinguish between needs and wants. You need food. You do not need restaurants. You need clothes. You do not need new clothes every month. You need shelter. You do not need cable TV. You need transportation. You do not need a car payment.

Most of what you think you need, you actually want. Wants are not bad. But wants come after needs. And when you are broke and in debt, wants come last.

Needs first. Savings second. Debt elimination third. Wants last. Get the order right.

The Strategy: Cut from the Bottom Up

When most people try to cut expenses, they start small. They cancel one streaming service. They skip coffee one day per week. They reduce their cable package. They save twenty or thirty dollars per month. Then they pat themselves on the back and think they are done.

That is not cutting expenses. That is nibbling around the edges. That saves you a few hundred dollars per year. That does not build wealth.

You need to cut aggressively. You need to cut from the bottom up. You need to eliminate entire categories of spending, not just reduce them slightly.

Here is the strategy: Go back to your one-month audit from Chapter 2. Look at your low priority expenses. Those are the expenses you classified as wants, not needs. Those are restaurants, entertainment, subscriptions, new clothes, coffee shops, impulse purchases.

Your goal is to reduce low priority expenses by eighty to ninety percent. Not ten percent. Not twenty percent. Eighty to ninety percent.

If you currently spend five hundred dollars per month on low priority expenses, your goal is to cut that to fifty to one hundred dollars per month. You eliminate four hundred to four hundred fifty dollars of waste. That is four thousand eight hundred to five thousand four hundred dollars per year. That is your emergency fund. That is your debt elimination. That is your down payment.

Most people say that is impossible. It is not impossible. It is uncomfortable. There is a difference.

Let me show you exactly what to cut and how to cut it.

Cut Housing Costs

Housing is usually your biggest expense. If your housing is more than thirty percent of your take-home income, you need to address it.

I know what you are thinking: "I have a lease" or "I just bought this house" or "I can't move right now." Fine. If your housing expense is truly fixed for the next six to twelve months, accept it and cut everything else more aggressively. But when your lease ends or when you have the opportunity to refinance or move, you must take action.

Here are your options for cutting housing costs.

Get a roommate. This is the fastest way to cut housing costs. If you pay twelve hundred dollars per month for rent and you get a roommate who pays six hundred dollars, your housing cost just dropped to six hundred dollars per month. You save seven thousand two hundred dollars per year. That is wealth-building money. Yes, you lose privacy. Yes, you have to share your space. Yes, you have to compromise on things like noise and cleanliness. Do it anyway. It is temporary. Most people refuse to get roommates because they value privacy over wealth. Those people stay broke. You value wealth over privacy. Get a roommate.

Move to a cheaper place. When your lease ends, move to a cheaper apartment. Not a slightly cheaper apartment. A significantly cheaper apartment. If you pay twelve hundred per month, move to a place that costs eight hundred or nine hundred per month. Save three hundred to four hundred dollars per month. That is three thousand six hundred to four thousand eight hundred dollars per year. "But I like where I live." You will like being debt-free and having savings more. "But the cheaper place is not as nice." You are not paying for nice. You are paying for shelter. Get shelter for less money.

Build wealth. Move back to a nicer place later when you can afford it.

<u>Move to a less expensive area.</u> If housing in your city is expensive, move to a less expensive city or a less expensive neighborhood. Commute farther if necessary. If rent in your current area is fifteen hundred per month and rent thirty minutes away is one thousand per month, move. Save five hundred per month. That is six thousand dollars per year. "But I don't want to commute." Then you do not want to build wealth. You want convenience over wealth. Those are your priorities. Fine. But do not complain about being broke. You are choosing to be broke.

<u>Refinance your mortgage.</u> If you own a home and interest rates have dropped since you bought, refinance. A refinance from a six percent rate to a four percent rate on a two hundred thousand dollar mortgage saves you about two hundred fifty dollars per month. That is three thousand dollars per year. Call lenders. Get quotes. If the numbers work, refinance. Stop paying more interest than necessary.

<u>Negotiate rent.</u> When your lease is up for renewal, negotiate with your landlord. Ask for a rent decrease or ask them to keep rent the same instead of raising it. Many landlords will negotiate to keep good tenants. The worst they can say is no. But if you do not ask, the answer is automatically no. Be willing to sign a longer lease if they give you a lower monthly rate. Two years at one thousand dollars per month is better than one year at one thousand one hundred dollars per month.

<u>Stop paying for storage units.</u> If you are paying for a storage unit, you are paying to store things you do not use. Sell what is in the storage unit. Donate what you cannot sell. Stop paying one hundred to two hundred dollars per month to store junk. That is twelve hundred to twenty-four hundred dollars per year you are wasting. Empty the unit. Cancel the rental. Keep the money.

Cut Transportation Costs

Transportation is usually your second biggest expense. This is where most people have the most waste. This is where you can save the most money the fastest.

Sell your car and buy a beater. I said this in Chapter 3. I will say it again here because it is that important. You cannot afford a car payment. Sell your car. Even if you owe more than it is worth. Even if you have to add money to the deal. Sell it. Buy a three thousand to eight thousand dollar car with cash. Drive an ugly car for two to three years while you build wealth. Then buy a nicer car with cash when you can afford it.

Here is the math one more time because people need to see it repeatedly before they believe it. You have a car worth twenty thousand dollars. You owe twenty-two thousand dollars. You are upside down by two thousand dollars. You sell the car for twenty thousand. You pay off the twenty-two thousand dollar loan. You owe the bank two thousand dollars. You set up a payment plan for that two thousand. You pay two hundred dollars per month for ten months to pay off the deficiency. Meanwhile, you save two thousand dollars. You buy a four thousand dollar car with cash. Your total out of pocket is four thousand dollars over ten months. After ten months, you have no car payment. You own a car outright. You went from four hundred dollar monthly car payments to zero car payments. You now have four hundred extra dollars per month to save or pay off other debt. That is four thousand eight hundred dollars per year.

"But what if the cheap car breaks down?" Budget one hundred dollars per month for repairs. Even with repairs, you are still ahead by three hundred dollars per month. "But I need a reliable car for work." A four thousand to eight thousand dollar car is reliable if you buy smart. Get a Honda or Toyota with high miles but a clean maintenance record. These cars run for two hundred thousand miles or more. Do your research. Have a mechanic inspect before you buy. You can find reliable transportation for less money. You just have to be willing to drive something that is not pretty.

Stop car washes. Wash your car at home. You do not need professional car washes. Buy a bucket, soap, and sponge for twenty dollars total. Wash your car yourself. If you currently pay twenty dollars twice per month for car washes, you save four hundred eighty dollars per year. That is not huge, but it adds up. Every dollar you do not waste is a dollar you can save.

Shop for cheaper car insurance. Call multiple insurance companies. Get quotes. You can often save two hundred to five hundred dollars per year by switching companies. Also raise your deductibles. If you have a five hundred dollar deductible, raise it to one thousand dollars. Your monthly premium drops. Yes, you pay more out of pocket if you have an accident. But if you drive carefully and rarely have accidents, you save money every month. Take that savings and put it in your emergency fund. If you do have an accident, you use your emergency fund to pay the deductible.

Reduce miles driven. Drive less. Combine errands into one trip. Carpool to work. Work from home if your employer allows it. Take public transportation. Ride a bike. Walk. Every mile you do not drive saves gas, reduces wear on your car, and lowers your maintenance costs. If you currently drive three thousand miles per month and you cut that to two thousand miles per month, you save gas and extend the life of your vehicle. Small changes add up.

Cancel roadside assistance plans. If you have AAA or a roadside assistance plan through your insurance or car manufacturer, cancel it. These cost fifty to one hundred dollars per year or more. If your car breaks down, call a local tow company. Pay the one-time fee. You will likely pay less over time than you pay for the annual membership. Or better yet, learn basic car maintenance. Learn how to change a tire, jump a battery, and add fluids. Handle minor issues yourself. Save the money.

Cut Food Costs

Food is where most people bleed money without realizing it. You did your audit in Chapter 2. You know how much you spend on food. Now you are going to cut that number dramatically.

Stewardship of Provision

God provides food. This is basic provision. But provision requires stewardship. When you waste food, you waste God's gift. When you spend excessively on food while claiming you cannot afford to save, you mismanage provision.

Proverbs 12:27 states: "Whoever is slothful will not roast his game, but the diligent man will get precious wealth." The slothful person wastes what they have. They let food spoil. They throw away leftovers. They spend money on convenience instead of investing time in preparation. The diligent person maximizes what they have. They use everything. They waste nothing. They build wealth through careful management.

Every dollar you waste on food is a dollar you cannot invest in your future. Every meal you throw away uneaten is provision squandered. God gave you income to steward. Food is part of that stewardship. Manage it well.

Stop eating out. I do not mean reduce eating out. I mean stop eating out. Zero dollars per month for restaurants. Zero dollars per month for fast food. Zero dollars per month for coffee shops. Zero dollars per month for food delivery apps. Pack every meal. Cook every meal at home. Bring coffee from home in a thermos. This is non-negotiable. Eating out is a luxury. You do not have luxuries right now. You are building wealth. Once you hit your financial goals, you can add restaurants back. But not now. If you currently spend four hundred dollars per month eating out and you cut that to zero, you save four thousand eight hundred dollars per year. That is massive.

"But I'm too busy to cook." No you are not. You watch TV three hours per night. You scroll social media two hours per day. You have time. You choose not to use it for cooking. Change your priorities. "But I don't know how to cook." Learn. YouTube has thousands of free cooking videos. Start with simple meals. Rice and beans. Pasta. Chicken and vegetables. You do not need to be a chef. You need to feed yourself for less money. "But I'll miss going out with friends." Invite friends to your house. Cook together. Have potlucks. Socialize without spending money at restaurants. If your friends only want to hang out at expensive restaurants, find new friends. Friends who support your financial goals are better than friends who pressure you to spend money you do not have.

Meal plan every week. Sit down every Sunday. Plan every meal for the week. Breakfast, lunch, dinner, snacks. Write down exactly what you will eat. Make a grocery list based on your meal plan. Buy only what is on the list. Do not deviate. Do not browse. Do not impulse buy. Get in, get your groceries, get out. Planning eliminates waste. When you plan, you buy only what you need. When you do not plan, you buy random items that sit in your pantry unused. You let produce rot in your refrigerator. You waste money.

Cook in bulk. Make large batches of food. Eat leftovers. Cook a whole chicken on Sunday. Eat chicken for dinner Sunday. Use leftover chicken for sandwiches Monday. Make chicken soup Tuesday. Use every bit. Cook a big pot of chili. Eat it for three days. Freeze half for next week. Cooking in bulk saves time and money. You cook once, eat multiple times. You buy ingredients in larger quantities for less per unit. You waste less food.

Buy generic everything. Store brand products cost twenty to forty percent less than name brands. Most are made by the same manufacturers in the same factories with different labels. Switch to generic for everything. Cereal, pasta, rice, canned goods, frozen vegetables, bread, milk, everything. If you currently spend six hundred dollars per month on groceries and you switch all name brands to generic, you save one hundred twenty to two hundred forty dollars per month. That is fourteen hundred forty to twenty-eight hundred eighty dollars per year. Try generic versions. If you truly hate a generic item, switch back to name brand for that one item. But try everything generic first. You will find most items are identical.

Cut meat consumption. Meat is expensive. Chicken breast is six to eight dollars per pound. Ground beef is five to seven dollars per pound. Steak is ten to twenty dollars per pound. Beans are one dollar per pound. Lentils are one dollar per pound. Eggs are three dollars per dozen. Reduce meat. Increase beans, lentils, eggs, and peanut butter. These are cheap protein sources. Have meatless meals three to four times per week. Use meat as a flavoring instead of the main dish. A little chicken goes a long way in a stir fry or soup. You do not need eight ounces of meat per meal. Most Americans eat too much meat anyway. Cut back. Save money. Improve your health.

Stop buying processed and packaged foods. Chips, cookies, crackers, frozen meals, pre-made snacks all cost more per serving than homemade versions. Buy ingredients, not products. Buy flour, sugar, oats, and make your own baked goods. Buy potatoes and make your own fries. Buy popcorn kernels and make your own popcorn for fifty cents instead of buying microwave popcorn for four dollars. Processed foods are convenient. Convenience costs money. You are not paying for convenience right now. You are paying off debt and building wealth.

Use every bit of food. Stop wasting food. Use vegetable scraps to make stock. Freeze overripe bananas for smoothies. Eat leftovers for lunch. Freeze leftovers if you cannot eat them within two days. Plan meals around what is already in your refrigerator and pantry. Before you go grocery shopping, use what you have. Waste is throwing money in the trash. Americans waste one hundred fifty billion dollars worth of food per year. You are not contributing to that statistic anymore. Use everything. Waste nothing.

Shop sales and use coupons. Check the weekly ad before shopping. Plan meals around what is on sale. If chicken is on sale, make chicken meals that week. If ground beef is on sale, make ground beef meals. Stock up on non-perishables when they are on sale. Rice on sale for half price? Buy six bags. Pasta on sale? Buy ten boxes. These items do not spoil. Use coupons for items you already buy. Do not buy something just because you have a coupon. Coupons are only savings if you were going to buy the item anyway.

Cut Utility Costs

Utilities are mostly fixed, but you have more control than you think. Small changes in usage create big savings over time.

Lower your thermostat in winter, raise it in summer. Set your heat to sixty-five degrees in winter. Wear sweaters and socks inside. Set your air conditioning to seventy-eight degrees in summer. Use fans. Your body adjusts after a few days. Every degree you lower the heat in winter or raise the air conditioning in summer saves three to five percent on your energy bill. If your energy bill is one hundred fifty dollars per month, adjusting the thermostat saves nine to fifteen dollars per month, which is one hundred eight to one hundred eighty dollars per year. Do this. Stop paying to heat and cool your house to uncomfortable levels. Adjust.

Unplug devices when not in use. Electronics and appliances draw power even when turned off. This is called phantom load or vampire power. Unplug phone chargers, laptop chargers, coffee makers, microwaves, TVs, gaming consoles when not in use. Or use power strips. Plug multiple devices into one power strip. Flip the switch on the power strip to cut power to everything at once. This saves five to ten percent on your electric bill. On a one hundred dollar monthly electric bill, that is five to ten dollars per month, which is sixty to one hundred twenty dollars per year.

Wash clothes in cold water. Ninety percent of the energy used to wash clothes goes to heating the water. Wash everything in cold water. Modern detergents work fine in cold water. Your clothes will be just as clean. This saves about fifty dollars per year on your energy bill. Also, air dry clothes instead of using the dryer. Hang clothes outside on a line if you can. Hang them inside on a drying rack if you cannot. The dryer is one of the most expensive appliances to run. Eliminating dryer use saves one hundred to two hundred dollars per year.

Take shorter showers. Cut your shower time in half. If you currently take ten-minute showers, take five-minute showers. Set a timer. Get in, wash, get out. A ten-minute shower uses twenty-five gallons of hot water. A five-minute shower uses twelve and a half gallons. Cutting shower time in half cuts your water heating costs significantly. If everyone in your household does this, you save fifty to one hundred dollars per year.

Fix leaks immediately. A dripping faucet wastes gallons of water per day. A running toilet wastes hundreds of gallons per day. Fix leaks as soon as you notice them. Toilet leak detection tablets cost five dollars. Drop one in your toilet

RUN YOUR HOUSEHOLD LIKE A BUSINESS 179

tank. If the water in the bowl turns color, you have a leak. Fix it. Leaks cost you money every day they go unfixed.

Cancel cable. Cable costs eighty to one hundred fifty dollars per month or more. You do not need cable. You have been told you need cable. You do not. Cancel it. If you must have TV, keep one streaming service. One. Not five. One. Netflix or Hulu or Disney Plus. Pick one and spend ten to fifteen dollars per month. Cancel the rest. If you currently spend one hundred twenty dollars per month on cable and you cancel it completely, you save fourteen hundred forty dollars per year. If you keep one streaming service for fifteen dollars per month, you still save twelve hundred sixty dollars per year. That is your emergency fund. That is your debt payment. Do not tell yourself you need cable. You need wealth more than you need cable.

Reduce your internet speed. Call your internet provider. Ask what speeds they offer. Most people pay for the fastest speed because faster sounds better. You do not need the fastest speed. You need enough speed to work from home if necessary and stream one show at a time. If you are paying for one gigabit speed and you downgrade to one hundred megabits, you save twenty to forty dollars per month. That is two hundred forty to four hundred eighty dollars per year. Your internet will still work fine for everything you actually do. You just will not be able to brag about your internet speed anymore. You do not need to brag. You need to save money.

Switch to a cheaper phone plan. You are paying too much for your phone. If you are with Verizon, AT&T, or T-Mobile, you are overpaying. Switch to a discount carrier. Mint Mobile, Cricket, Metro by T-Mobile, Visible, Google Fi, all offer service for fifteen to forty dollars per month. These carriers use the same networks as the big carriers. Same coverage. Same reliability. Lower price. If you are paying eighty dollars per month for your phone and you switch to a thirty-dollar plan, you save fifty dollars per month, which is six hundred dollars per year. Do this today. Call a discount carrier. Port your number. Save money.

Stop paying for phone insurance. Phone insurance costs eight to fifteen dollars per month. That is ninety-six to one hundred eighty dollars per year. Over two years, you pay one hundred ninety-two to three hundred sixty dollars for insurance. If you break your phone, the insurance has a deductible of fifty to two hundred dollars. So you pay for insurance and you still pay a deductible if you make a claim. This is a bad deal. Cancel phone insurance. Be careful with your phone. Put it in a case. Use a screen protector. If you break your phone, buy a used phone on eBay or Swappa for one hundred to three hundred dollars. You will likely spend less over time than you spend on insurance.

Cut Entertainment and Subscription Costs

Entertainment and subscriptions are pure waste when you are broke and in debt. These are luxuries. Cut them.

Cancel all streaming services except one. You have Netflix, Hulu, Disney Plus, HBO Max, Amazon Prime Video, Apple TV Plus, Paramount Plus, Peacock, ESPN Plus. You are paying eighty to one hundred twenty dollars per month for streaming services. Cancel all of them except one. If you must have TV, keep one service. Watch what is on that service. When you finish everything you want to watch, cancel it and subscribe to a different service for one month. Rotate. Never pay for more than one service at a time. Better yet, cancel all of them. Read books from the library. Listen to podcasts. Watch free content on YouTube. You do not need paid entertainment. Entertainment is what broke people buy to distract themselves from being broke. Stop distracting yourself. Face your situation. Build wealth. Enjoy entertainment later when you can afford it.

Cancel your gym membership. You do not need a gym.

Run outside. Do pushups at home. Do situps at home. Watch free workout videos on YouTube. Bodyweight exercises are free. Gyms cost thirty to seventy dollars per month. If you pay fifty dollars per month for a gym and you cancel it, you save six hundred dollars per year. "But I need the gym to stay motivated." No you do not. You need discipline to stay motivated. Discipline is free. If you cannot work out without a gym, you will not work out with a gym either. You are paying for the feeling of being someone who goes to the gym, not for actually going to the gym. Stop paying for feelings. Cancel the membership. Work out at home.

Cancel magazine subscriptions. You do not read them. They pile up unread. You look at the pictures occasionally. That is not worth ten to thirty dollars per year per subscription. Cancel them. If you want to read magazines, go to the library. Read them for free. Same content. Zero cost.

Stop going to movies. Movie tickets cost ten to fifteen dollars per person. Popcorn and drinks add another fifteen to twenty dollars. A movie for two people costs forty to fifty dollars. That is insane. Wait for movies to come to streaming or rent them for five dollars. Watch at home. Make popcorn at home for fifty cents. Same entertainment. Ninety percent lower cost. If you go to movies twice per month and you stop, you save eighty to one hundred dollars per month, which is nine hundred sixty to twelve hundred dollars per year.

Cancel music streaming services. If you pay for Spotify or Apple Music, cancel it. Use the free version with ads. Or listen to free music on YouTube. Or listen to the radio. Or buy songs you love for ninety-nine cents each and own them forever instead of renting access for ten dollars per month. Music streaming is ten to fifteen dollars per month, which is one hundred twenty to one hundred eighty dollars per year. Save that money.

Quit hobbies that cost money. If your hobby requires spending money every week or every month, quit the hobby temporarily. Golf costs forty to one hundred dollars per round. Quit golf. Pick up running. Running shoes cost fifty dollars and last six months. That is eight dollars per month. Photography costs thousands for gear and hundreds for prints and editing software. Put the camera away. Read books about photography instead. Learn without spending. Any hobby that requires ongoing spending needs to pause while you build wealth. Pick up free hobbies. Read. Write. Draw. Hike. Walk. Exercise. Cook. These cost nothing or almost nothing.

Stop buying books. Use the library. Every book you want to read is at the library. Free. You do not need to own books. You need to read books. Reading is free at the library. If you currently buy five books per month at fifteen dollars each, you spend seventy-five dollars per month, which is nine hundred dollars per year. Go to the library. Save nine hundred dollars per year.

Cut Personal Care Costs

Personal care is another area where people spend far more than necessary. You need to be clean and presentable. That does not cost much.

Get cheaper haircuts. If you pay fifty to one hundred dollars for haircuts, stop. Go to a barber school or a budget haircut place. Great Clips, Supercuts, Sport Clips all charge fifteen to twenty-five dollars. Barber schools charge ten dollars or less. Your hair will look fine. Nobody cares about your haircut as much as you think they do. If you currently get haircuts every three weeks at sixty dollars and you switch to a twenty-dollar haircut every four weeks, you save about four hundred eighty dollars per year.

Cut your own hair. Even better, learn to cut your own hair or have a family member cut it. Buy clippers for thirty dollars. Watch YouTube videos. Cut your own hair at home. Free haircuts forever after the initial thirty-dollar investment. If you get twelve haircuts per year at twenty dollars each, you spend two hundred forty dollars per year. Buy clippers once for thirty dollars. Save two hundred ten dollars per year every year after.

Stop getting your nails done. If you get manicures and pedicures, stop. Paint your own nails. Buy nail polish for five dollars. Use it twenty times. That is twenty-five cents per use versus thirty to sixty dollars per salon visit. If you get your nails done twice per month at forty dollars per visit, you spend eighty dollars per month, which is nine hundred sixty dollars per year. Paint your own nails. Save nine hundred fifty dollars per year.

Cancel spa services and massages. You do not need massages. You want massages. There is a difference. If you are getting regular massages, facials, or other spa services, stop. These cost fifty to one hundred fifty dollars per visit. Pure luxury. Save that money. If you need relaxation, take a hot bath at home. Free.

Stop dying your hair. If you dye your hair at a salon, stop. Let your natural color show. Or dye it at home. Home hair dye costs eight to fifteen dollars and lasts three months. Salon color costs one hundred to three hundred dollars and lasts three months. If you color your hair at a salon four times per year at one hundred fifty dollars, you spend six hundred dollars per year. Switch to home dye at twelve dollars four times per year. You spend forty-eight dollars. Save five hundred fifty-two dollars per year. Or stop coloring altogether. Embrace your natural hair. Save six hundred dollars per year.

Cut Clothing and Shopping Costs

Americans buy too many clothes. You have enough clothes. Stop buying more.

Stop buying clothes for six months. Implement a clothing ban. Zero dollars spent on clothes for six months. You have clothes in your closet right now. Wear them. When something wears out completely, then and only then do you replace it. Buy one replacement item from a thrift store or clearance rack. Then go back to buying nothing. Most people can go six to twelve months without buying any new clothes. Try it. If you currently spend one hundred fifty dollars per month on clothes and you stop for six months, you save nine hundred dollars. Put that toward your emergency fund or debt.

Shop thrift stores only. When you must buy clothes, shop thrift stores. Goodwill, Salvation Army, local thrift shops. You can find name brand clothes in excellent condition for three to eight dollars per item. Shirts, pants, dresses, jackets, shoes, everything. If you need work clothes, thrift stores have them. If you need casual clothes, thrift stores have them. The only difference is the clothes are not brand new. They have been worn by someone else. Who cares? Wash them. Wear them. Save money. If you spend fifty dollars per month on new clothes and you switch to thrift stores spending fifteen dollars per month, you save thirty-five dollars per month, which is four hundred twenty dollars per year.

Stop buying shoes. You do not need new shoes every few months. Buy one good pair of shoes. Wear them until they fall apart. Then buy another good pair. If you currently buy shoes every other month at sixty dollars per pair, you spend three hundred sixty dollars per year on shoes. Buy one pair per year at sixty dollars. Save three hundred dollars.

Stop buying accessories and jewelry. Belts, scarves, watches, necklaces, earrings, rings, bracelets. You do not need any of this. You have enough accessories. Stop buying more. If you spend thirty dollars per month on accessories, you spend three hundred sixty dollars per year. Stop. Save three hundred sixty dollars per year.

Sell clothes you do not wear. Go through your closet. Pull

out everything you have not worn in six months. Sell it. Poshmark, eBay, Facebook Marketplace, local consignment shops. Turn unused clothes into cash. Use that cash to fund your emergency fund. Most people have hundreds of dollars worth of clothes sitting unused in their closets. Liquidate. Get the money. Stop holding onto things you do not use.

Cut Gift and Holiday Spending

Gifts are where many budgets explode. People go into debt buying gifts for people who do not need more stuff. Stop.

Set a strict gift budget. Decide how much you will spend on gifts for the entire year. Fifty dollars per month is six hundred dollars per year. That is your total gift budget. Birthdays, Christmas, weddings, baby showers, everything comes from that six hundred dollars. When the money is gone, you are done giving gifts. No exceptions. No credit cards. No borrowing from other categories. Done.

Make gifts instead of buying them. Baked goods cost five to ten dollars to make and people love them. Photo albums with printed pictures cost ten to twenty dollars. Handmade crafts cost little to nothing if you use materials you already have. Your time and effort mean more than expensive store-bought items. Make gifts. Save money. Give from the heart, not from the wallet.

Give experiences instead of things. Offer to babysit for new parents. Offer to help someone move. Offer to cook dinner for someone. Offer your time and skills. These gifts cost nothing but time. They are often more valuable than physical items. Nobody needs more stuff. Everyone needs help and support.

Agree with family on gift limits. Talk to your extended family. Propose a twenty-five dollar per person limit for Christmas. Or propose doing a name draw where each adult buys for one other adult instead of everyone buying for everyone. Many families will be relieved to reduce gift expectations. Everyone feels the pressure. Nobody wants to be the first to suggest spending less. Be the first. Start the conversation.

Stop buying gifts for coworkers and acquaintances. You do not need to buy gifts for everyone you know. You do not need to participate in every office gift exchange. You do not need to buy teacher gifts and coach gifts and neighbor gifts. These are optional. Opt out. Save your money. True friends and family will understand. If someone judges you for not buying them a gift, they are not someone who deserves your money or your attention.

Cut Miscellaneous and Hidden Costs

There are dozens of small expenses hiding in your budget. These add up to hundreds or thousands per year. Find them. Cut them.

Cancel monthly subscriptions you do not use. Go through your bank statements and credit card statements. Look for recurring monthly charges. Magazine subscriptions, app subscriptions, software subscriptions, delivery services, monthly boxes of any kind. Cancel anything you have not used in the past month. If you are not using it weekly, you do not need it. Cancel it. Most people have five to ten subscriptions they forgot about. At ten dollars each, that is fifty to one hundred dollars per month, which is six hundred to twelve hundred dollars per year.

Stop paying bank fees. If your bank charges monthly fees, switch banks. Plenty of banks and credit unions offer free checking accounts with no monthly fees, no minimum balance requirements, and no overdraft fees if you opt out of overdraft protection. Move your money to a free bank. Stop giving banks ten to thirty-five dollars per month for the privilege of holding your money.

Stop paying ATM fees. Use your bank's ATMs only. Or get cash back at grocery stores when you shop. Never use out-of-network ATMs that charge three to five dollars per transaction. If you use an ATM twice per week at four dollars per transaction, you spend four hundred sixteen dollars per year on ATM fees. That is insane. Plan ahead. Get cash from your bank. Stop paying fees.

Eliminate late fees and overdraft fees. Pay bills on time. Set up auto-pay for bills so you never miss a due date. Track your bank balance so you never overdraft. Late fees and overdraft fees are thirty to thirty-five dollars each. If you get hit with one fee per month, you waste three hundred sixty to four hundred twenty dollars per year. These fees are completely avoidable. Avoid them.

Stop buying lottery tickets and scratch-offs. You are not going to win. The lottery is a tax on people who cannot do math. If you buy ten dollars in lottery tickets per week, you spend five hundred twenty dollars per year. You will never see that money again. Stop buying lottery tickets. Put that ten dollars per week in your emergency fund. In one year, you will have five hundred twenty dollars that actually exists instead of a pile of losing tickets.

Stop smoking and drinking. Cigarettes cost seven to ten dollars per pack. A pack-a-day smoker spends twenty-five hundred to thirty-six hundred dollars per year on cigarettes. Alcohol costs vary, but people who drink regularly spend one hundred to three hundred dollars per month, which is twelve hundred to thirty-six hundred dollars per year. Quit smoking. Quit drinking. Improve your health. Save thousands per year. This is not just a financial decision. This is a life decision. But the financial impact is massive.

Stop buying convenience store snacks. Every time you stop for gas, you go inside and buy a drink and snacks for five to ten dollars. If you do this twice per week, you spend five hundred twenty to one thousand forty dollars per year on convenience store junk. Stop going inside. Pay at the pump. Leave immediately. Keep snacks and water in your car. Stop impulse buying.

The Aggregate Impact of Cutting

Let me show you what happens when you cut aggressively across all categories.

Here is a typical budget before cuts:

- Housing: $1,200 (no change, lease locked in)
- Utilities: $200
- Transportation: $550 (car payment + insurance + gas)
- Groceries: $400
- Eating out: $300
- Entertainment: $120 (streaming + movies + hobbies)
- Personal care: $100
- Clothing: $100
- Gym: $50
- Gifts: $50
- Subscriptions: $50
- Miscellaneous: $80

Total monthly expenses: $3,200

Now here is the same budget after aggressive cutting:

- Housing: $1,200 (unchanged for now, but plan to get roommate or move)
- Utilities: $140 (cut $60 by lowering thermostat, unplugging devices, shorter showers)
- Transportation: $250 (sold car with payment, bought beater, cheap insurance)

- Groceries: $280 (cut $120 by meal planning, buying generic, cutting meat)
- Eating out: $0 (cut $300 completely)
- Entertainment: $15 (cut $105, kept one streaming service only)
- Personal care: $30 (cut $70 by getting cheap haircuts, no salon services)
- Clothing: $0 (cut $100, six month clothing ban)
- Gym: $0 (cut $50, work out at home)
- Gifts: $25 (cut $25 by making gifts, setting strict limits)
- Subscriptions: $0 (cut $50, canceled everything)
- Miscellaneous: $20 (cut $60, eliminated impulse purchases and fees)

Total monthly expenses: $1,960

You cut from $3,200 to $1,960. You eliminated $1,240 per month in waste. That is $14,880 per year.

What does fourteen thousand eight hundred eighty dollars per year do?

- Fully fund a starter emergency fund of $2,000 in less than two months
- Pay off $14,880 in debt in one year
- Save a $14,880 down payment in one year
- Or split it: Save $7,440 in emergency fund and pay off $7,440 in debt in one year

You go from broke with no savings and debt to having savings and eliminating debt in one year. You do this not by making more money (though you should also do that), but by cutting ruthlessly.

Most people will say these cuts are too extreme. Most

people will say they cannot live like this. Most people will make excuses.

Those people stay broke.

You will make these cuts. You will live like this temporarily. You will build wealth that lasts permanently.

When People Push Back

You will face resistance when you cut expenses. Some resistance will come from yourself. Most will come from others.

Family will tell you that you are being cheap. Friends will tell you that you are no fun anymore. Your spouse will tell you that life is too short to live like this. Coworkers will pressure you to go out to lunch. People will judge your choices.

Let them judge. You are building wealth. They are building debt. You will retire early. They will work until they die. You will have options. They will have stress. You win. They lose.

Here is what you say when people push back:

"I'm focusing on my financial goals right now." Do not explain further. Do not justify. State your boundary. Change the subject.

"I'm saving for a house." Most people understand this. They will still judge, but they will judge less. Use this response if you need social acceptance.

"I can't afford it." This is honest. People who care about you will respect this. People who do not respect this are not people you need in your life.

Say no without apology. "No, I'm not going to dinner." "No, I'm not buying that." "No, I'm not participating in the gift exchange." No is a complete sentence. You do not owe anyone an explanation. Say no. Move on.

Find friends who support your goals. If your current friends pressure you to spend money, find new friends. Join free meetup groups. Find people at church or community centers. Find people who are also building wealth or who do not define friendship by spending money together. True friends support your goals. Everyone else is an acquaintance or an obstacle.

The Timeline

How long do you need to live like this? Six to twelve months minimum. Longer if your debt is significant or your income is low.

This is not forever. This is temporary. You are making a short-term sacrifice for a long-term benefit.

After six to twelve months of aggressive cutting, you will have built habits. You will have eliminated waste. You will have your emergency fund started or fully funded. You will have made significant progress on debt.

At that point, you can add a few things back if you want. Maybe you add back one hobby that costs money. Maybe you start eating out once per month. Maybe you buy a few new clothes.

But you will not add everything back. Because by that point, you will realize you do not miss most of what you cut. You will realize you were wasting money on things that added no value to your life. You will choose to keep living below your means because living below your means is what built your wealth.

Your Assignment for This Chapter

Do not move to Chapter 6 until you complete this assignment:

1. Review your one-month audit from Chapter 2. Identify every low priority expense. List them all.
2. Go through the cutting strategies in this chapter. For

each category, write down specifically what you will cut and how much you will save.

3. Calculate your total monthly savings from cutting. Write down this number. This is how much extra you will have for savings and debt elimination every month.

4. Make the cuts this week. Do not wait. Cancel subscriptions today. Call your insurance company today. Implement the changes now.

5. Track your spending for the next month. Verify that you actually cut what you said you would cut. If you failed to cut something, cut it immediately.

6. After thirty days, review your results. How much did you actually save? Did you stick to zero eating out? Did you cancel all subscriptions? Did you avoid buying clothes? Be honest. If you failed anywhere, recommit and try again.

7. After sixty days, review again. Is it getting easier? Have new habits formed? Are you feeling less deprived? Most people report that month two is much easier than month one.

8. After ninety days, evaluate whether you need to cut more or whether you can sustain the current level. If you are not hitting your savings goals, cut more. If you are hitting your goals, maintain the cuts.

9. Do not add expenses back until you have a fully funded emergency fund and all non-mortgage debt eliminated. Do not reward yourself for three months of cutting by going back to wasteful spending. Stay disciplined until you hit your goals.

10. Once you hit your goals, decide intentionally what to add back. Do not add everything back. Add only what genuinely improves your life. Keep the rest eliminated.

Cutting expenses is painful. Staying broke is more painful. Choose the temporary pain that leads to permanent wealth over the permanent pain that leads nowhere.

Do the work. Cut aggressively. Build wealth.

CHAPTER 6
AVOIDING THE 17 SERIOUS BUDGET MISTAKES

Most people don't fail financially because they lack intelligence. They fail because they underestimate how predictable their patterns are. A budget can be well-designed, biblically grounded, and logically sound—and still collapse if the same repeating behaviors are allowed to operate unchecked.

That's why this chapter matters.

If Chapter 4 gave you a money blueprint and Chapter 5 taught you how to prune waste, this chapter is about protection. It is the guardrail chapter. It is where you learn to recognize the traps that quietly sabotage households—especially households that have sincere intentions and strong goals.

Over the years, I've watched the same mistakes show up across income levels, across professions, across family structures. The difference between families who build wealth and families who stay stuck is rarely knowledge alone. It is consistency, self-awareness, and the willingness to correct small errors before they become large consequences.

So I'm going to lay these mistakes out plainly—not to shame you, but to sharpen you. When you can name a problem, you can govern it. When you can anticipate a trap, you can avoid it.

As you read these mistakes, don't treat them like accusations. Treat them like diagnostics. If you recognize yourself in one of them, that's not failure—that's awareness. Awareness is power. The goal is not perfection. The goal is progress with fewer self-inflicted setbacks.

To make this easier to absorb, I'm grouping the mistakes into themes. That way you can see not just what went wrong, but why it went wrong.

Planning Mistakes

The first category of mistakes happens before the month even begins. These are the errors of assumption—planning based on hope instead of reality, underestimating what life costs, or failing to assign money intentionally before the pressure of the month starts making decisions for you. A weak plan creates a weak month.

Mistake 1: Not Estimating How Much You Spend

The first and most fundamental mistake is not knowing where your money goes. You think you spend four hundred dollars per month on groceries. You actually spend seven hundred. You think you spend one hundred fifty dollars per month eating out. You actually spend four hundred. You think you spend fifty dollars per month on subscriptions. You actually spend one hundred fifty.

Your budget is based on estimates instead of facts. Your estimates are wrong. Your budget fails before it begins.

This is why Chapter 2 exists. This is why you must do the one-month audit. You cannot build a budget on guesses. You cannot allocate money you do not have. You cannot cut expenses you have not identified.

People resist the audit because tracking every dollar for thirty days feels tedious. They tell themselves they already know their spending. They create budgets based on what they think they spend instead of what they actually spend. Then they wonder why their budget never works.

The audit reveals the truth. The truth is uncomfortable. But the truth is also necessary. You cannot fix what you cannot see. The audit shows you what to see.

If you skipped Chapter 2 and jumped straight to budget creation, go back now. Do the audit. Track every dollar for thirty days. Build your budget on facts, not estimates. This fixes mistake number one.

Mistake 2: Forgetting to Save for the Unexpected

The second mistake is planning for everything except the things you cannot plan for. Your budget includes rent, utilities, groceries, gas, insurance, debt payments. Your budget accounts for every expected expense. Your budget has no room for the unexpected.

Then your car breaks down. The repair costs eight hundred dollars. You have no money for the repair. You put it on a credit card. You go into debt. Your budget is destroyed. You give up.

Or your child needs glasses. Two hundred fifty dollars. Credit card. Debt. Budget destroyed.

Or your dog gets sick. Veterinarian bill is four hundred dollars. Credit card. Debt. Budget destroyed.

Or your water heater fails. Replacement costs twelve hundred dollars. Credit card. Debt. Budget destroyed.

Unexpected expenses are not actually unexpected. They are inevitable. Cars break. Appliances fail. People get sick. Emergencies happen. The only surprise is that people are surprised when these things occur.

Your budget must include savings for unexpected

expenses. This is your emergency fund. This is the ten percent of income you allocate to emergency savings every single month in Chapter 3. This is non-negotiable.

The emergency fund is what prevents unexpected expenses from destroying your budget. Car breaks down? Use emergency fund. Budget stays intact. Replenish emergency fund next month. Move forward.

Without an emergency fund, every unexpected expense becomes a crisis. With an emergency fund, unexpected expenses are merely inconveniences. You handle them. You continue. You build wealth.

Start building your emergency fund immediately if you have not already. Even if you can only save fifty dollars per month, start. Build a one thousand dollar starter emergency fund as fast as possible. Then keep building to three months of expenses. Then six months. Then twelve months.

The emergency fund is what separates people who survive financial setbacks from people who get destroyed by them. Build the fund. Protect your budget.

Mistake 3: Having Unrealistic Expectations

The third mistake is expecting immediate perfection. You create your first budget. You expect to follow it perfectly. You expect to never overspend. You expect to hit all your goals in month one.

Then reality arrives. You overspend on groceries by fifty dollars. You forgot about a birthday gift. You had an unexpected expense you did not budget for. Your first month is not perfect.

So you give up. You tell yourself budgeting does not work. You abandon the system. You go back to having no budget and no plan.

This is the wrong response. Your first budget will not be perfect. Your second budget will not be perfect. Your tenth budget might not be perfect. Budgeting is a skill. Skills require practice. Practice requires failure.

The goal is not perfection. The goal is progress. If you overspent by five hundred dollars last month and you only overspent by two hundred dollars this month, that is progress. If you forgot to budget for three expenses last month and you only forgot one this month, that is progress. If you saved nothing last month and you saved fifty dollars this month, that is progress.

Celebrate progress. Learn from mistakes. Adjust your budget based on what you learned. Try again next month. Keep improving.

Most people quit after one or two months because their budget was not perfect. They had unrealistic expectations. They expected immediate success with no learning curve. They were wrong.

Give yourself six months to get good at budgeting. Six months of making mistakes, learning, adjusting, improving. By month six, your budget will work smoothly. By month twelve, budgeting will feel natural. By month twenty-four, you will wonder how you ever lived without a budget.

But you must push through the first few imperfect months. Lower your expectations. Focus on progress, not perfection. Stay committed. The results come.

Mistake 4: Budgeting Based on Your Gross Income

The fourth mistake is building your budget on money you never see. You make five thousand dollars per month gross income. You build your budget assuming you have five thousand dollars to allocate. You create spending categories. You allocate money. Your budget adds up perfectly.

Then you get paid. Your paycheck is thirty-seven hundred dollars after taxes, insurance, and retirement contributions. You do not have five thousand dollars. You have thirty-seven hundred dollars. Your budget is based on money that does not exist. Your budget fails immediately.

This mistake seems obvious, but people make it constantly. They look at their salary and think that is their income. They forget about taxes. They forget about insurance premiums. They forget about retirement contributions. They budget money they will never touch.

Your budget must be based on take-home income. This is the money that actually hits your bank account. This is the money you can actually spend and save. This is the only income that matters for budgeting purposes.

Look at your paycheck. Find the net pay amount. That is your take-home income. That is the number you use for budgeting. If your paycheck varies because you work hourly or earn commissions, use your lowest monthly take-home from the past six months. Budget conservatively. If you make more, use the extra for savings or debt. Never budget based on your best month.

Some people argue they should budget based on gross income because taxes and insurance are expenses. They are wrong. Taxes and insurance come out before you see the money. You cannot spend money that never reaches your account. You budget what you actually have, not what you theoretically earned.

Fix this mistake by using take-home income for all budget calculations. Your allocation percentages in Chapter 3 are based on take-home income. Your savings goals are based on take-home income. Everything is based on take-home income. Get this right or your budget will never work.

Mistake 5: Not Considering Cheaper Alternatives

The fifth mistake is accepting your current costs as fixed and unchangeable. You pay one hundred fifty dollars per month for internet. You put that in your budget. You never question whether you could pay less. You pay eighty dollars per month for your phone. You budget eighty dollars. You never shop for a cheaper plan. You pay six hundred dollars per month for car insurance. You budget six hundred. You never get quotes from other companies.

Your budget locks in waste. Your budget assumes you cannot do better. Your budget accepts overpaying as normal.

Every expense in your budget should be questioned. Every expense should be challenged. Every expense should be evaluated for cheaper alternatives. This is especially true for recurring monthly expenses because small savings compound over time.

Internet service is a perfect example. Most people pay for faster speeds than they need. You pay for one gigabit internet because faster sounds better. You actually need one hundred megabits for everything you do. Downgrading saves thirty dollars per month, which is three hundred sixty dollars per year. You never notice the speed difference. You save the money.

Phone service is another example. You pay eighty dollars per month with a major carrier. You could switch to a discount carrier using the same network for thirty dollars per month. Same coverage. Same reliability. Lower price. You save fifty dollars per month, which is six hundred dollars per year. But you stay with the expensive carrier because you always have. You never consider alternatives.

Insurance is another example. You have the same car insurance company you signed up with five years ago. You never shop for better rates. You could save two hundred to five hundred dollars per year by getting quotes from multiple companies. Takes thirty minutes. Saves hundreds of dollars. But you never do it because your current insurance is on autopay. You forget it exists. You overpay for years.

Go through every line item in your budget. Ask yourself if a cheaper alternative exists. Call competitors. Get quotes.

Compare prices. Switch if you can save money. Repeat this process every year. Prices change. Your situation changes. Better deals appear. Capture the savings.

Most people can cut their monthly expenses by two hundred to four hundred dollars just by shopping for cheaper alternatives on services they already use. That is twenty-four hundred to forty-eight hundred dollars per year. That is your emergency fund. That is your debt elimination. That is your wealth building. But you have to look for the savings. They do not find you.

Stop accepting your current costs as unchangeable. Challenge every expense. Find cheaper alternatives. Save the difference. Build wealth.

Pause here and notice the pattern: these mistakes are rarely dramatic. They are small, repeated, and justified. They sound like, "It's just this once," or "We'll make it up next month," or "I deserved it," or "We had no choice." This is how financial drift works. It does not announce itself. It slowly normalizes the exception until the exception becomes the lifestyle.

This is why awareness is so valuable. When you catch drift early, you correct it cheaply. When you let it run for years, it becomes expensive.

Execution Mistakes

Some people build a decent plan and then abandon it in real time. Execution mistakes are not intellectual—they are behavioral. They show up in the middle of the month when a small deviation becomes a new habit. A plan you don't follow is not a plan. It is a wish.

Mistake 6: Buying Too Much House

The sixth mistake is spending too much on housing. This

is the single biggest budget destroyer I see. People buy or rent homes they cannot afford. They stretch their budget to the breaking point. They tell themselves they deserve it. They convince themselves they will make more money in the future. They ignore the math.

Your housing should be twenty-five to thirty percent of your take-home income. Maximum. If your housing is more than thirty percent, you are house poor. You are spending too much on shelter and not enough on everything else. Your budget has no flexibility. You cannot save. You cannot invest. You live paycheck to paycheck even if you make good money.

The Spiritual Reality: Shelter Is Provision, Not Identity

God provides shelter as a gift. You need a place to live. Scripture acknowledges this basic need. But Scripture also warns against seeking security in houses rather than in God.

Proverbs 24:27 instructs: "Prepare your work outside; get everything ready for yourself in the field, and after that build your house." First establish your economic foundation. Then build your dwelling. Do not invert this order. Do not build beyond your means and then struggle to sustain it.

Jesus taught His disciples not to worry about where they would live or what they would wear. Matthew 6:31-33 states: "Therefore do not be anxious, saying, 'What shall we eat?' or 'What shall we drink?' or 'What shall we wear?' For the Gentiles seek after all these things, and your heavenly Father knows that you need them all. But seek first the kingdom of God and his righteousness, and all these things will be added to you."

Your house is shelter, not identity. Your house is provision, not status. Your house should serve your mission, not define your worth. When you spend 40-50% of your income on housing to impress others or to feel successful, you violate this principle. You seek identity in your house rather than in God. You sacrifice your financial future for a temporary feeling of accomplishment.

God cares that you have shelter. God does not care if your shelter impresses your neighbors. Spend what you need for safe, functional housing. Do not spend what you want to project an image of success. The image is false. The financial damage is real.

Here is what happens when you buy too much house. You make five thousand dollars per month take-home. You buy a house with a mortgage payment of two thousand dollars per month. That is forty percent of your income. You have three thousand dollars left for everything else. Utilities, transportation, food, insurance, debt payments, savings, everything must come from three thousand dollars. The math does not work. You cannot save. You go into debt for unexpected expenses. You are one emergency away from disaster.

The bank approved you for the mortgage. The bank said you could afford it. The bank was wrong. Banks approve people for mortgages they cannot afford all the time. Banks look at debt-to-income ratios and credit scores. Banks do not care if you can save money or build wealth. Banks care if you can make the monthly payment. Do not trust the bank's approval amount. Trust the math.

If you already bought too much house, you have limited options. You can increase your income dramatically. You can take on roommates to split housing costs. You can rent out part of your house on Airbnb. You can sell the house and buy something cheaper even if you take a loss. Or you can stay in the expensive house and accept that you will never build wealth until you fix your housing cost.

Most people choose the last option. They stay in the expensive house. They make excuses. They tell themselves they will make more money soon. They tell themselves they need the space. They tell themselves their kids need to stay in the same school. They choose the house over wealth. They stay broke.

If you have not bought a house yet, do not make this

mistake. Keep your housing at twenty-five to thirty percent of take-home income. Buy less house than the bank says you can afford. Leave room in your budget for savings, investments, and unexpected expenses. Choose wealth over square footage.

The house you live in does not build wealth unless you sell it and downsize. The house you live in is an expense, not an investment. Minimize this expense. Maximize your wealth building.

Mistake 7: Not Tracking Your Actual Expenses

The seventh mistake is creating a budget and then ignoring it. You build a beautiful budget. You allocate every dollar. You set spending limits for each category. You feel accomplished. Then you never look at it again.

You spend money throughout the month. You do not track whether you are staying within your budget categories. You do not check if you overspent on groceries or eating out or entertainment. You assume everything is fine. You hope you stayed on budget.

End of the month arrives. Your bank account is empty. You have no idea where the money went. Your budget predicted you would have five hundred dollars left over. You have zero. What happened?

You created a budget but you did not track your spending against the budget. The budget was a plan. You did not execute the plan. You did not monitor whether you followed the plan. The budget failed because you ignored it.

A budget without tracking is worthless. A budget is not a one-time document you create and forget. A budget is a living tool you use daily. You track every expense as it happens. You compare your spending to your budget limits. You adjust behavior when you approach your limits. You course-correct before you overspend.

This is why the cash envelope system from Chapter 3 works so well. Cash envelopes force tracking. You allocate cash to each spending category. You see how much is left in each envelope. When the envelope is empty, you stop spending in that category. Tracking is automatic and visual.

If you do not use cash envelopes, you must track digitally. Use a budget app that links to your bank accounts. Check it daily. Review your spending every Sunday. Make sure you are staying within budget in each category. If you are overspending in one category, cut spending in another category to compensate. Do not wait until the end of the month to discover you failed.

Tracking takes five minutes per day. Check your budget app in the morning. Check again at night. Compare actual spending to budgeted amounts. That is it. Five minutes per day prevents budget failure.

Most people spend hours creating budgets and zero minutes tracking them. Reverse this. Spend thirty minutes creating your budget. Spend five minutes per day tracking it. The tracking is what makes the budget work. Without tracking, you are budgeting blind. You will fail.

Mistake 8: Neglecting Emergency Planning

The eighth mistake is having no plan for emergencies. This is related to mistake number two but worse. Not only do you fail to save for emergencies, you also fail to plan for what you will do when emergencies happen.

Your car breaks down. You need eight hundred dollars for repairs. You have no emergency fund. What do you do? You have no plan. You panic. You put it on a credit card. You go into debt. Your budget is destroyed.

If you had planned for emergencies, you would have known exactly what to do. You would have had options. You would have had a decision tree. Car breaks down?

First, check emergency fund. If emergency fund is insufficient, use option two: ask family for a short-term loan. If that fails, use option three: sell something to raise cash. If that fails, use option four: take on extra work to earn the money quickly. If that fails, use option five: negotiate a payment plan with the mechanic. Credit card is the last resort, not the first option.

Planning for emergencies means thinking through scenarios before they happen. What would you do if you lost your job tomorrow? How would you pay rent? How long would your emergency fund last? What expenses would you cut immediately? What extra income could you generate? Who could you ask for help? These are questions you answer before you need the answers. This is emergency planning.

Planning for emergencies also means having insurance for major catastrophes. Health insurance, car insurance, homeowners or renters insurance, life insurance if you have dependents. These insurances are expensive. They are also necessary. One major uninsured emergency can bankrupt you. One car accident without insurance. One house fire without insurance. One medical emergency without insurance. These events destroy decades of wealth building in one day.

Do not skip insurance to save money. Insurance is not optional. Insurance is one of your high priority expenses from Chapter 2. You pay for insurance before you pay for anything else. Protect yourself from catastrophic loss.

Most people have no emergency plan. They hope nothing bad happens. They avoid thinking about worst-case scenarios. Then the worst happens. They have no plan. They make terrible decisions under pressure. They destroy their financial progress.

Create your emergency plan today. Write down what you would do in various emergency scenarios. Build your emergency fund. Buy necessary insurance. Sleep better knowing you are prepared. Do not wait for the emergency to arrive unprepared.

Mistake 9: Forgetting to Allow for Non-Recurring Expenses

The ninth mistake is budgeting only for monthly expenses and forgetting about expenses that happen less frequently. You budget for rent, utilities, groceries, gas, insurance. These are monthly expenses. You remember them. You plan for them.

But you forget about car registration that happens once per year. You forget about annual insurance premiums. You forget about property taxes if you own a home. You forget about holiday spending. You forget about birthday gifts. You forget about back-to-school shopping. You forget about annual subscriptions. You forget about quarterly pest control. You forget about semi-annual dental visits.

These expenses are predictable. They happen every year. But because they do not happen every month, you forget to budget for them. Then they arrive. You have no money set aside. You use money from other budget categories. You overspend. Your budget fails.

The solution is to convert non-recurring expenses into monthly budget line items. Car registration costs two hundred forty dollars per year. Divide by twelve. Twenty dollars per month. Budget twenty dollars per month for car registration. Save it every month in a separate account. When the bill comes, you have the money waiting.

Holiday spending is five hundred dollars per year. Divide by twelve. Forty-two dollars per month. Budget forty-two dollars per month for holidays. Save it every month. When December comes, you have five hundred dollars ready. No credit cards. No debt. No budget destruction.

Go through your calendar for the past year. List every non-monthly expense. Car registration, insurance premiums, property taxes, holiday gifts, birthday gifts, back-to-school items, annual subscriptions, quarterly services, anything that happens less than monthly. Add up the annual cost of each item. Divide by twelve. Those are your monthly savings amounts for non-recurring expenses.

Add these amounts to your budget as monthly line items. Treat them like any other monthly expense. Save the money every month. When the expense arrives, you are prepared.

Most people treat non-recurring expenses as unexpected surprises. They are not surprises. They are predictable. Plan for them. Budget for them. Save for them. Remove the surprise.

Mistake 10: Not Expecting the Really Bad Stuff

The tenth mistake is planning for small emergencies but not planning for catastrophic events. You have a two thousand dollar emergency fund. That covers most small emergencies. Car repair, appliance replacement, minor medical bills. You feel prepared.

Then you lose your job. Your emergency fund covers two weeks of expenses. You are unemployed for four months. Your emergency fund is gone in two weeks. You have fourteen more weeks with no income and no money. You burn through all your savings. You go into massive debt. You lose everything.

Or you have a major medical emergency. Hospital stay. Surgery. Weeks of recovery. Even with insurance, your out-of-pocket costs are ten thousand dollars. Your emergency fund covers twenty percent of the bill. You go into debt for the rest. Your financial progress is destroyed.

Or your car is totaled in an accident. Insurance covers some of the value. You still owe five thousand dollars on the loan. You need to buy another car. You do not have the money. You go into debt.

These are catastrophic events. Small emergency funds do not cover catastrophic events. This is why Chapter 3 recommends building a full emergency fund of six to twelve months of expenses. Not six to twelve hundred dollars. Six to twelve months of expenses. For most people, that is fifteen thousand to forty thousand dollars.

Most people think that amount is impossible. Most people stop at one or two thousand dollars and call it done. Then catastrophe strikes. They are not prepared. They lose everything.

You must plan for the really bad stuff. Job loss. Major medical emergency. Catastrophic car or home damage. Disability. Death of a spouse. These events happen. They are rare, but they are not impossible. You need financial protection against them.

Build a full emergency fund of six to twelve months of expenses. This takes time. This might take two to five years. That is acceptable. Keep building. Keep saving. Get to full funding. This fund is what prevents catastrophic events from destroying your life.

Also, make sure you have adequate insurance. Health insurance with a manageable out-of-pocket maximum. Car insurance with actual coverage, not just minimum liability. Homeowners or renters insurance with replacement value coverage. Disability insurance if your income depends on your ability to work. Life insurance if people depend on your income.

Insurance and emergency funds work together. Insurance covers truly massive expenses like fifty thousand dollar hospital bills. Emergency funds cover smaller catastrophes like job loss or major car repairs. Together, they protect you from the really bad stuff.

Do not ignore catastrophic risk. Do not assume bad things only happen to other people. Plan for the really bad stuff.

Build the big emergency fund. Buy the insurance. Protect yourself and your family.

Pause here and notice the pattern: these mistakes are rarely dramatic. They are small, repeated, and justified. They sound like, "It's just this once," or "We'll make it up next month," or "I deserved it," or "We had no choice." This is how financial drift works. It does not announce itself. It slowly normalizes the exception until the exception becomes the lifestyle.

This is why awareness is so valuable. When you catch drift early, you correct it cheaply. When you let it run for years, it becomes expensive.

Emotional and Behavioral Mistakes

This is where budgets get personal. Money is never just math —it is identity, anxiety, desire, ego, comparison, and comfort. If your emotional life is unmanaged, your spending will reflect it. These mistakes don't come from spreadsheets; they come from pressure.

Mistake 11: Not Budgeting Your Top Resource: Time

The eleventh mistake is budgeting your money but not budgeting your time. You carefully track every dollar. You know exactly where your money goes. But you have no idea where your time goes.

Time is more valuable than money. You can always make more money. You cannot make more time. Time is your most limited resource. Yet most people manage it poorly.

You say you have no time to cook, so you eat out and waste four hundred dollars per month. But you watch TV three hours per night. You have time. You choose to spend it on TV instead of cooking.

You say you have no time to work a side job to make extra

income. But you scroll social media two hours per day. You have time. You choose to spend it on social media instead of making money.

You say you have no time to exercise, so you pay for a gym membership you do not use. But you browse the internet for an hour every morning. You have time. You choose to spend it browsing instead of exercising.

Your time choices affect your money. When you waste time, you waste money. When you manage time well, you save money and make money.

This is why Chapter 4 starts with a time audit. You must know where your time goes before you can redirect it to wealth-building activities. Most people waste twenty to thirty hours per week on activities that produce no value. Those hours could be spent cooking to save money, working a side job to make money, or learning skills to increase future income.

Budget your time the same way you budget your money. Allocate time to high-priority activities first. Sleep, work, essential personal care, essential family time, essential household tasks. These are non-negotiable. Then allocate time to wealth-building activities. Cooking, side income, skill development, exercise for health. These activities improve your financial situation. Finally, allocate remaining time to entertainment and relaxation. These activities are important for mental health but should not dominate your schedule.

Track your time for one week using the method from Chapter 4. See where it actually goes. Compare that to where you want it to go. Make changes. Redirect wasted time to productive activities. Watch your financial situation improve.

People who budget only money will always struggle. People who budget both time and money will build wealth faster and more sustainably. Budget both resources. Master both. Build wealth.

Mistake 12: Owning Too Many Financial Accounts

The twelfth mistake is having accounts everywhere. You have three checking accounts at different banks. You have five savings accounts. You have seven credit cards. You have two brokerage accounts. You have retirement accounts at three previous employers. You have accounts you forgot you opened.

You think more accounts means better organization. You think separate accounts for separate purposes makes sense. Vacation account. Emergency account. Christmas account. Car repair account. House down payment account. Separate account for everything.

This creates complexity. This creates confusion. This makes budgeting harder, not easier. You cannot see your complete financial picture. You forget about accounts. You lose track of money. You waste time managing multiple accounts. You pay unnecessary fees. You fail to meet minimum balance requirements. You let accounts go dormant.

Simplicity is better. Consolidate your accounts. One checking account for all expenses. One savings account for your emergency fund. One savings account for other goals if you must separate them. One or two credit cards maximum. One brokerage account for investments. Consolidate old retirement accounts into one current account.

Fewer accounts means better visibility. You can see everything in one place. You know exactly how much money you have. You can track spending more easily. You make better decisions because you have complete information.

Some people argue that multiple accounts help them mentally separate money for different purposes. This is psychological, not financial. You do not need separate physical accounts to mentally separate money. You can track different savings goals in a spreadsheet or budget app while keeping the money in one account. You get the psychological benefit without the complexity.

The only exception is keeping your emergency fund in a separate account from your regular savings. Emergency fund should be slightly difficult to access so you are not tempted to raid it for non-emergencies. Put it in a different bank or a savings account without a debit card. But beyond that one separation, consolidate everything else.

Review all your financial accounts today. Close accounts you do not need. Consolidate accounts where possible. Simplify your financial life. Make budgeting easier. Reduce complexity. Build wealth more efficiently.

Mistake 13: Spreading Yourself Too Thin

The thirteenth mistake is trying to achieve too many financial goals simultaneously. You want to save for retirement. You want to build an emergency fund. You want to pay off debt. You want to save for a house down payment. You want to save for your kids' college. You want to take a vacation. You want to buy a new car. You want everything at once.

So you allocate small amounts to each goal. Fifty dollars to retirement. Fifty dollars to emergency fund. Fifty dollars to debt. Fifty dollars to house fund. Fifty dollars to college fund. Fifty dollars to vacation fund. You are making progress on everything. You are mastering nothing. Nothing gets fully funded. Nothing gets completed. You spread yourself too thin.

Years pass. Your retirement account has four thousand dollars. Your emergency fund has three thousand dollars. Your debt is barely smaller. Your house down payment fund has five thousand dollars. Your college fund has two thousand dollars. You have a little bit of everything and not enough of anything. You cannot retire. Your emergency fund is inadequate. Your debt still controls you. You cannot buy a house. You cannot pay for college. You have no vacation.

This approach fails because achieving financial goals requires focus. You must prioritize. You must attack one or two goals at a time. You must fully fund or fully eliminate before moving to the next goal.

Here is the correct priority order for most people:

First priority: Build a starter emergency fund of one thousand to two thousand dollars. Stop. Do nothing else until this is done. Focus everything on this goal. Get it done in one to three months.

Second priority: Pay off all non-mortgage debt using the debt snowball method from Chapter 3. Put every extra dollar toward your smallest debt. Pay it off. Move to the next debt. Repeat until all consumer debt is eliminated. This might take one to three years. Focus on this goal until completion.

Third priority: Build a full emergency fund of six to twelve months of expenses. Redirect all the money you were putting toward debt into your emergency fund. Build it to full funding. This might take one to three years. Focus on this goal until completion.

Fourth priority: Save for your next major goal. House down payment. Kids' college. Whatever matters most to you. Now you can split your savings between this goal and retirement contributions. You have no debt. You have a full emergency fund. You have bandwidth for multiple goals.

This sequential approach feels slower. You are only working on one or two goals at a time instead of seven goals. But sequential actually gets you to your goals faster because you are not spreading resources too thin. You fully complete each goal before moving forward.

Most people try to do everything at once. They make minimal progress on everything. They complete nothing. They get discouraged. They quit. They start over. They waste years.

You will focus. You will prioritize. You will attack one goal at a time. You will complete each goal before moving forward. You will actually achieve your financial objectives instead of perpetually working toward them.

Identify your top financial priority today. Focus all extra money on that one goal. Ignore other goals until your top priority is complete. Then move to the next priority. Sequential focus builds wealth. Spreading thin builds frustration.

Mistake 14: Never Adjusting Your Variable Expenses

The fourteenth mistake is setting your budget once and never adjusting it. You allocate three hundred dollars per month for groceries. You spend three hundred dollars per month for six months. Then grocery prices increase due to inflation. You still try to spend three hundred dollars per month. You cannot. You overspend by fifty dollars. Your budget fails.

Or your income increases. You get a raise. Your take-home goes from four thousand to forty-five hundred dollars per month. You keep using your old budget designed for four thousand per month. You do not adjust your allocations. You do not increase your savings percentage. You just spend the extra five hundred dollars on whatever. Your budget becomes irrelevant.

Or your life situation changes. You get married. You have a baby. You move to a new city. Your expenses change dramatically. You keep using your old budget. Your budget no longer matches reality. You stop following it.

Your budget is not a static document you create once and follow forever. Your budget is a living tool that changes as your life changes. You must review and adjust regularly.

Review your budget every month. Did you overspend in any category? Increase the allocation for next month or commit to spending less. Did you underspend in any category? Decrease the allocation and redirect the money to savings or debt. Did any unexpected expenses occur? Add a budget line for them going forward if they might recur.

Review your budget quarterly. Has your income changed? Adjust your allocation amounts proportionally. Have prices increased significantly? Adjust your spending category amounts to match reality. Have your goals changed? Adjust your savings allocations accordingly.

Review your budget annually. Major life changes. Job changes. Family changes. Housing changes. These require complete budget overhauls. Do not use last year's budget if your life is dramatically different this year.

Your variable expenses should decrease over time as you get better at budgeting and cutting waste. If your grocery allocation stays the same year after year, you are not improving. You should be finding ways to reduce costs. You should be getting more efficient. Your variable expenses should shrink while your savings rate increases.

Some people create a budget in January and never look at it again. They wonder why it stops working by March. Your budget only works if you maintain it. Review monthly. Adjust when needed. Keep your budget aligned with reality. This is maintenance. Maintenance is not optional.

Mistake 15: Forgetting to Balance Your Checking Account

The fifteenth mistake is not tracking your checking account balance. You know roughly how much money you have. You know you got paid last week. You know you paid some bills. You think you have enough money. You hope you have enough money. You guess you have enough money.

Then you buy groceries for one hundred fifty dollars. Your debit card declines. You check your account. You have seventy-five dollars. You overdrew your account yesterday and did not know it. Now you owe a thirty-five dollar overdraft fee. You transfer money from savings to cover the shortage. You pay another fee for the transfer. You wasted sixty to seventy dollars because you did not know your account balance.

Or worse, you write several checks without tracking your balance. They all clear on the same day. Each one overdrafts. You owe five overdraft fees at thirty-five dollars each. One hundred seventy-five dollars in fees because you did not track your balance. That is your grocery money gone.

This mistake seems ancient. People assume online banking and apps eliminate the need to balance checking accounts. They assume they can just check their balance on their phone and know exactly what they have. They are wrong.

Your online balance includes pending transactions that have not cleared yet. You bought gas yesterday for forty dollars. The charge is pending. Your online balance does not reflect it. You think you have more money than you actually have. You spend based on the incorrect balance. You overdraft.

Your online balance does not include checks you wrote that have not been cashed yet. You wrote a two hundred dollar check to your landlord on the first. Today is the fifth. The check has not cleared. Your online balance still shows that two hundred dollars. You spend it. The check clears on the sixth. You overdraft.

You must balance your checking account manually. Track every transaction. Subtract each transaction from your balance immediately when you make it. Know your true available balance at all times. Do not rely on your bank's online balance. It is not accurate until all transactions clear.

Many people stopped balancing their checking accounts when debit cards became common. They stopped writing checks. They assumed swiping a card meant instant balance updates. They were wrong. Some transactions take days to clear. Gas stations pre-authorize fifty dollars even if you only pump twenty dollars. The extra thirty dollars is tied up for days. Hotels pre-authorize more than your room cost. Restaurants process the tip later. Online purchases take days to process.

Balance your account in a check register, a spreadsheet, or a budget app. Record every transaction immediately. Deduct it from your available balance immediately. Compare your records to your bank statement monthly. Reconcile discrepancies. Know your true balance always.

Overdraft fees are completely avoidable. They are a tax on people who do not track their money. Stop paying this tax. Balance your account. Know your balance. Never overdraft again. Save hundreds of dollars per year in unnecessary fees.

Mistake 16: Not Using Budgeting Software

The sixteenth mistake is trying to budget entirely in your head or on scraps of paper. You create rough mental budgets. You have a general idea of your spending limits. You try to remember if you spent too much in any category this month. You estimate your remaining balance. You guess whether you can afford something.

Mental budgeting does not work. You cannot track dozens of transactions and multiple spending categories in your head. You forget what you spent. You underestimate totals. You confuse which expenses came from which month. Your mental budget is inaccurate. You overspend without realizing it. Your budget fails.

Paper budgeting is slightly better but still fails for most people. You write your budget on paper. You manually write down every expense. You manually add up totals. You do math by hand. This works if you have extreme discipline and good handwriting and patience for arithmetic. Most people do not. They start strong. They stop tracking after two weeks. The paper disappears. The budget dies.

Software solves these problems. Budgeting apps and spreadsheets automate calculations. They track your spending for you if you link bank accounts. They categorize transactions automatically. They show you instantly if you are over budget in any category. They remove the friction from budgeting.

Tracking becomes easy. You open your app once per day. You review transactions. You make sure everything is categorized correctly. Done. Five minutes. The app does the math. The app shows you pretty charts. The app tells you if you are on track.

Some people resist budgeting software. They worry about security. They do not want to link their bank accounts to an app. They prefer doing everything manually. Fine. Use a spreadsheet. Create your budget in Excel or Google Sheets. Enter your transactions daily. Let the spreadsheet do the math. This is better than mental or paper budgeting.

But linking to a budgeting app is better. The security concerns are mostly unfounded. Good budgeting apps use bank-level encryption. They do not store your bank login information. They use secure APIs to read your transactions. The risk is minimal. The benefit is massive. Automatic transaction tracking means you actually track instead of forgetting.

Choose a budgeting tool and commit to it. Mint, YNAB, EveryDollar, Monarch, Copilot, any tool from that transcript you shared earlier. Pick one. Learn it. Use it daily for ninety days before switching. Give it time to work.

People who use budgeting software succeed at rates far higher than people who do not. The software removes friction. The software makes tracking easy. The software makes budgeting sustainable. Use software. Stop relying on your memory. Stop doing math by hand. Let technology help you build wealth.

Mistake 17: Trying to Keep Up with Friends

The Spiritual Disease: Pride, Comparison, and Coveting

Keeping up with others is not a financial problem. Keeping up with others is a spiritual problem. The tenth commandment forbids it: "You shall not covet your neighbor's house... or anything that is your neighbor's." (Exodus 20:17)

When you spend money trying to match someone else's lifestyle, you are coveting. You are saying their life looks better than yours. You are saying God's provision for you is insufficient. You are rejecting God's unique plan for your life in favor of someone else's path.

Pride drives comparison. You want to be seen as successful. You want to be perceived as wealthy. You want admiration. So you spend money you do not have to create an image that is not real. You build a house of cards that collapses under the weight of debt.

First Timothy 6:6-10 warns: "But godliness with contentment is great gain, for we brought nothing into the world, and we cannot take anything out of the world. But if we have food and clothing, with these we will be content. But those who desire to be rich fall into temptation, into a snare, into many senseless and harmful desires that plunge people into ruin and destruction. For the love of money is a root of all kinds of evils."

The love of money drives comparison. The love of appearance drives overspending. The love of status drives debt. These loves destroy you spiritually before they destroy you financially.

Contentment is the antidote. Contentment says "I have what I need. I do not need what others have. God provides for me according to His plan, not according to my neighbor's income." Contentment breaks the comparison trap. Contentment frees you from the bondage of other people's opinions.

Galatians 6:4-5 instructs: "Each one should test their own actions. Then they can take pride in themselves alone, without comparing themselves to someone else, for each one should carry their own load." Your financial journey is yours alone. Your progress is measured against your goals, not against your neighbor's kitchen renovation.

The people you compare yourself to are probably broke. The expensive car has a massive payment attached. The big house has a crushing mortgage. The exotic vacations are charged to credit cards. The designer clothes are masking an empty bank account. You are competing to fail faster than people who are already failing.

Stop competing. Stop comparing. Stop coveting. Run your race. Build your wealth. Honor God with your resources. Let others do what they want. You do what is right.

Your friends go out to dinner every weekend. You go with them. They spend sixty dollars per person on dinner and drinks. You spend sixty dollars too. You cannot afford sixty dollars. You do it anyway because everyone else is doing it.

Your coworkers all have new cars. You drive a ten-year-old car. You feel embarrassed. You buy a new car you cannot afford. You take on a car payment you do not need. You go into debt to match your coworkers.

Your neighbors renovate their kitchen. Granite countertops. New appliances. Custom cabinets. Their kitchen looks amazing. Your kitchen looks dated. You renovate your kitchen even though it works fine. You spend twenty thousand dollars you do not have. You take out a home equity loan. You go into debt to match your neighbors.

Your sister goes on expensive vacations. Hawaii. Europe. Cruises. She posts pictures on social media. You feel like a failure because you stay home. You book a vacation you cannot afford. You put it on credit cards. You go into debt to keep up with your sister.

This pattern destroys budgets and destroys wealth. You let other people's financial decisions dictate your financial decisions. You spend money trying to appear successful instead of actually building success. You buy things to impress people who do not care about you and who are probably broke themselves.

Here is the truth: Most people are broke. Most people live paycheck to paycheck. Most people are in debt. Most people have no savings. Most people will never retire comfortably. These are the people you are trying to keep up with. These are the people whose lifestyles you are copying. You are copying failure.

The people who appear most wealthy are often the most broke. The person with the expensive car has a massive car payment. The person with the big house is house poor. The person taking exotic vacations is drowning in credit card debt. The person wearing designer clothes has no emergency fund. They look successful. They are failing financially. You are competing to fail faster than they are.

Stop competing. Stop comparing. Stop trying to keep up. Your financial situation is your financial situation. Their financial situation is their financial situation. Their choices have nothing to do with your goals.

Your friends want to go out to dinner every weekend? Decline. Invite them over instead. Cook at home. Save the money. If they judge you for this, they are not real friends.

Your coworkers have new cars? Good for them. You have a paid-off car and money in savings. You win. They have car payments and no savings. They lose. Ignore them. Drive your old car. Build wealth.

Your neighbors renovated their kitchen? Their problem. Your kitchen works. Your money is in your emergency fund and retirement accounts. Their money is in cabinets that do not increase their net worth. You are smarter. Stop comparing.

Your sister goes on expensive vacations? She is probably broke. You are building wealth. You will be able to afford real vacations later when you have actual money. She will be working until she dies because she spent her retirement money on trips in her thirties.

The people who build real wealth do not try to look wealthy. They drive old cars. They live in modest homes. They do not care what other people think. They do not waste money trying to impress anyone. They save. They invest. They build net worth. They retire early. They win.

You will follow their path, not the path of people trying to look rich. You will stop competing with people who are broke. You will stop letting other people influence your spending. You will make financial decisions based on your goals, not other people's opinions.

Unfollow people on social media who make you feel inadequate. Stop spending time with people who pressure you to overspend. Find friends who support your financial goals. Surround yourself with people who are building wealth, not people who are faking wealth.

Your wealth is silent. Your progress is invisible to others. You are getting richer while they are getting poorer. Keep it that way. Let them judge. Let them wonder why you do not spend money. Meanwhile, you are building a financial foundation they will never have.

The Common Thread in All These Mistakes

These seventeen mistakes seem different on the surface. They cover different aspects of budgeting from tracking to planning to psychology. But they share a common thread: They all stem from lack of awareness and lack of discipline.

You make these mistakes when you do not pay attention to your money. You make these mistakes when you do not track consistently. You make these mistakes when you value short-term comfort over long-term wealth. You make these mistakes when you let emotions and other people control your financial decisions.

The solution to all seventeen mistakes is the same: Increase awareness and increase discipline. Pay attention to your money. Track everything. Plan ahead. Adjust when needed. Ignore outside pressure. Stay focused on your goals. Build systems that make good decisions automatic.

Most people make multiple mistakes from this list simultaneously. They do not track spending. They forget about non-recurring expenses. They spread themselves too thin. They try to keep up with friends. They make four or five mistakes at once. Their budgets never work. They never understand why.

You will be different. You will recognize these mistakes when you make them. You will fix them immediately. You will learn from them. You will not repeat them. This is what separates people who build wealth from people who stay broke.

Your Assignment for This Chapter

Review the seventeen mistakes in this chapter. Be honest with yourself about which mistakes you are currently making. Most people make at least five to seven of these mistakes. That is normal. You are not alone. You are not uniquely bad with money. You just have not learned these lessons yet.

Write down the mistakes you are making:

1. Which of the seventeen mistakes do I currently make?
2. Which mistake is costing me the most money?
3. Which mistake is easiest to fix immediately?
4. Which mistake will require the most work to fix?

Then create an action plan. Start with the mistake that is easiest to fix and the mistake that costs the most money. Fix those two mistakes this week. Then move to the next mistakes. Work through the list systematically. Do not try to fix all seventeen mistakes at once. That is spreading yourself too thin, which is mistake number thirteen. Fix two mistakes per month. In nine months, you will have eliminated all seventeen mistakes. Your budget will work flawlessly. You will build wealth consistently.

Share your mistake list with your accountability partner. Tell them which mistakes you are working on. Ask them to check your progress monthly. Accountability prevents backsliding. Your partner keeps you honest. Your partner reminds you of your commitment. Use them.

Most people will read this chapter and do nothing. They will recognize themselves in these mistakes. They will nod their heads. They will tell themselves they will fix it eventually. Eventually it never comes. Those people continue making the same mistakes for years. They stay broke.

The purpose of this chapter is not to make you afraid of mistakes. It is to make you resilient. Wealth is not built by people who never stumble. It is built by people who recover quickly, correct honestly, and refuse to repeat the same patterns.

If you take this seriously, something powerful happens: your budget stops being fragile. It becomes durable. Your system begins to hold under pressure, not just when everything is calm.

Now that you have the blueprint, the pruning, and the mistake-avoidance awareness, the next step is execution at scale—using tools to support consistency and connect your daily decisions to long-term wealth.

That is what Chapter 7 is about: tools, systems, and the wealth connection—how discipline becomes ownership, how order becomes opportunity, and how the Power Budget becomes a lifestyle, not a moment.

You will do the work. You will fix the mistakes. You will build a budget that works. You will avoid the mistakes that destroy wealth. You will build the wealth that lasts.

CHAPTER 7
TOOLS AND THE WEALTH CONNECTION

Tools do not create wealth. Systems do. That distinction matters, because many people believe that if they just find the right app, the right spreadsheet, or the right software, their financial life will finally fall into place. It won't. Tools do not fix discipline problems. They do not replace decision-making. They do not create commitment.

What tools can do—when used correctly—is support a system that already exists.

This chapter is about that connection. It is about how the daily discipline you've been building throughout this book translates into something tangible: stability, ownership, investing, and eventually legacy. The tools you choose are simply the bridge between intention and execution. They help you see clearly, act consistently, and stay accountable.

When tools are treated as the solution, people drift. When tools are treated as servants of the system, wealth compounds.

You have your foundation. You tracked your spending. You built your budget. You allocated your money. You made more income. You cut your expenses. You avoided seventeen serious mistakes.

Now you need tools. Now you need systems that make budgeting easier, more efficient, and more sustainable. Now you need to understand how the discipline you have built connects to lasting wealth.

This chapter provides the practical tools that support your budget and explains why budgeting discipline creates wealth that lasts for generations. Most people think budgeting is about restriction. Most people think budgeting is about suffering through a tight financial life. Most people miss the bigger picture.

Budgeting is not about restriction. Budgeting is about building wealth. The discipline you develop through consistent budgeting is the same discipline that creates millionaires. The habits you build by tracking every dollar are the same habits that build financial empires. The sacrifices you make now compound into freedom later.

This chapter gives you the tools you need and shows you where those tools are taking you. Let me start with the most practical question: what software and resources should you use to make budgeting work?

Before we talk about specific tools, it's important to understand the role they play. In business, tools support strategy; they do not define it. A company chooses software based on how it operates, not the other way around. Your household should do the same.

The right tool is not the most popular one. It is the one that matches your behavior, your level of complexity, and your willingness to engage consistently. A simple system you use beats a sophisticated system you ignore.

With that in mind, tools fall into three broad categories: tracking tools, planning tools, and automation tools. Each serves a different function, and together they create momentum.

Budgeting Tools and Software

I need to be direct about something before I recommend any tools. I do not endorse any particular budgeting software. I have no financial relationship with any of the companies I will mention. I do not receive commissions or kickbacks for recommending their products. I am not telling you which specific tool to use.

What I do endorse is this: investing in budgeting tools that help you achieve your financial goals. Whether you spend zero dollars on a free app or one hundred dollars per year on premium software does not matter to me. What matters is that you use something. What matters is that you track consistently. What matters is that you have a system that works for you.

The tool is not the solution. You are the solution. The tool just makes your work easier. A hammer does not build a house. A carpenter with a hammer builds a house. You are the carpenter. The budgeting tool is just the hammer. Pick a good hammer. Then do the work.

With that said, here are the budgeting tools available to you. I have organized them into categories based on functionality and price point. Research the ones that seem interesting. Try the ones that offer free trials. Pick one. Commit to using it for at least ninety days before switching. Ninety days is the minimum time needed to build habits and see if a tool actually works for your situation.

Premium Full-Service Budgeting Apps

These apps cost money, usually fifty to one hundred dollars per year or more. They offer comprehensive features including automated transaction tracking, investment monitoring, bill management, and detailed financial health snapshots. They are designed for people who want everything in one place and are willing to pay for convenience and power.

Monarch Money costs about one hundred dollars per year or fifteen dollars per month. It offers strong day-to-day budgeting features and incorporates investments into your larger financial picture. The interface is clean and customizable. You can share finances easily with a partner or financial advisor. The main drawback is the price point and some banking institutions do not connect well with the platform. No credit monitoring is included despite the premium price. Limited cryptocurrency support. Highly rated by users with over sixteen thousand reviews averaging 4.9 stars.

YNAB (You Need A Budget) costs about one hundred dollars per year. This is a zero-based budgeting app where every dollar gets assigned a job. The user interface is excellent and easy to navigate. You can share your subscription with up to five people in your household. It compiles historical spending data to show you trends and habits over time. The initial setup can be overwhelming for new users. The hands-on approach requires consistent engagement. Many users find it worth the price because it fundamentally changes how they think about money.

Copilot costs ninety-five dollars per year or thirteen dollars per month. Currently only available on Apple devices and only in the United States. The interface is exceptionally clean and intuitive. It learns your recurring expenses and anticipates them automatically. Customization options are nearly limitless. Bank account syncing is fast and reliable. It creates an overall budget with subcomponents that feed into the main budget. Many users consider this the best budgeting app available despite the platform limitations. Strong user reviews and high satisfaction ratings.

These premium apps are worth considering if you want powerful features, extensive customization, and minimal manual work. The cost is justified if the app actually helps you save significantly more money than you would save without it. If a one hundred dollar app helps you save an extra two thousand dollars per year through better tracking and awareness, the investment paid for itself twenty times over.

Mid-Tier Budgeting Apps

These apps cost between thirty and eighty dollars per year. They offer solid budgeting features without all the bells and whistles of premium apps. They balance functionality with affordability.

1. **EveryDollar** costs about eighty dollars per year. Created by Dave Ramsey, this is a zero-based budgeting app with a clean interface and good customization for categories. It integrates with Ramsey's Baby Steps system if you follow his program. The requirement to manually input every expense helps you stay aware of spending. The free version is barely usable. The paid version is expensive for what it offers compared to other apps at similar price points. Strong following among Ramsey fans but the price-to-features ratio is not competitive. Consider this if you are already following Dave Ramsey's system. Otherwise, better options exist at this price.

2. **Buddy** costs about fifty dollars per year. Straightforward income minus expenses budgeting. Pleasant user interface. Easy to share budgets with others. Bank connectivity provides near real-time transaction views. Seven-day free trial available. Some users report occasional bank connectivity issues. Does not include robust investment tracking

or credit score monitoring. Good middle-ground option for people who want automation without paying premium prices. Fair value for the cost.

3. **PocketGuard** costs about seventy-five dollars per year or thirteen dollars per month. Designed specifically for debt payoff. Sets payment schedules to help you eliminate debt by target dates. Partners with bill negotiation services to reduce recurring expenses. The free version is extremely limited with only two budget categories and no manual transaction entry. You need the paid version to get real functionality. Custom categories and splitting transactions across categories requires premium. The bill negotiation feature is built into the price, making this more expensive than pure budgeting apps. Decent if debt payoff is your primary focus. Otherwise, overpriced for basic budgeting needs.

4. Simplifi by Quicken costs about thirty-six dollars per year. Powered by Quicken. Relatively inexpensive. Outputs substantial data if you are a Quicken user already. The major drawback is you cannot even see the interface without providing your email and password upfront. No visible free trial. You get charged for a year on day one with unclear refund policies if you cancel early. This felt predatory during testing. The user experience is unfriendly. For the same price, better alternatives exist that respect users more. Not recommended despite the low cost.

These mid-tier apps work for people who want some automation and good features without spending premium prices. The sweet spot is usually forty to sixty dollars per year. Below that, you often sacrifice too much functionality. Above that, you might as well pay for premium apps that do more.

Budget-Friendly and Free Apps

These apps cost very little or nothing. They offer basic to moderate functionality. They work well for people just starting with budgeting or people who prefer simplicity over comprehensive features.

1. GoodBudget uses the digital envelope system. The free version is nearly identical to the paid version with minor restrictions. You can register a household and sync across devices. The envelope system is easier to understand initially than zero-based budgeting. All inputs are manual since it does not link to bank accounts. Does not offer holistic financial health tracking. Just pure budgeting. Simple and effective for people who want straightforward envelope budgeting. Good price-to-value ratio. Well-reviewed by users.

2. Spendee costs about twenty-three dollars per year. Everything you need for basic day-to-day money tracking. Simple and eye-pleasing interface. Wallets can be shared with others. Alerts and reminders prevent missed payments. Some users report bugs on Android devices. Does not sync with all bank accounts, so check compatibility before committing. Limited customization compared to premium apps. But what it commits to doing, it does well. Delivers more value than the price suggests. Good option for people who want clean, simple tracking without premium costs.

3. Today's Budget Money Tracker is a relatively new app with under three hundred ratings but excellent reviews. Day-to-day budget tracker that shows you how much you have to spend each day. You enter your total money available, track daily expenses, and it calculates your daily spending allowance. Deliberately does not link to bank accounts to keep things simple. Easy to do recurring expenses. Apple Watch capability. Clean, intuitive interface. Basic budgeting is extremely easy. Pleasant surprise during testing. Worth downloading for a weekend trial to see if the simple approach works for you.

4. Spending Tracker is free with optional paid features at three dollars. Less bubbly, more business-focused tracking. Input income and deduct expenses as you go. The free version covers most needs. Watch ads for premium features or pay once to remove ads and get extras. Good customization including dark mode and icon changes. Exports to Excel. Set up multiple accounts and alerts. Comprehensive for a free app while embracing its own limitations. Great for anyone trying to understand where money goes without paying for software.

5. Weple has a free version with ads or paid version for about seven dollars to remove ads and get more flexibility. Friendly interface with simple features. Just categorize money into expenses and income. Decent middle-of-the-road free option. Nothing spectacular but gets the job done for basic tracking.

6. Expenses OK costs about two dollars to add income tracking to the free expense-only version. Clean interface and intuitive design. Input expenses

throughout the day and see charts. Some customization available. Does not track long-term expenses or investments. The goal is just helping you be more conscientious about daily spending. No-frills money tracking at minimal cost.

7. Fleur costs about ten dollars for lifetime access or use the free version. Manual entry only, no bank account linking. Simple budgeting features with pie charts and bar graphs. The paid version adds more customization and features. Solid middle-of-the-road app. Lifetime purchase option is appealing for people who hate subscriptions.

Free and budget-friendly apps work well for people who want to start budgeting without financial commitment. Try several free options. See which interface you prefer. Commit to one for ninety days. If you outgrow it, upgrade to a mid-tier or premium app. But start somewhere. Starting with a free app is infinitely better than not starting at all.

Apps to Avoid

Not every budgeting app is worth your time. Some apps are poorly designed. Some are overpriced for what they deliver. Some have predatory practices. Some are not actually budgeting apps despite calling themselves that. Here are apps that did not make the recommended list and why.

1. Rocket Money claims to be a budgeting app but primarily focuses on subscription cancellation services. You cannot access any features without immediately linking a checking account. The budgeting features are secondary to their subscription management business. Not intuitive.

Poor user experience. Feels like bait-and-switch marketing. Skip this one.

2. NerdWallet is free but makes money by pushing credit cards, loans, insurance, and financial products to users. You are the product, not the customer. To use any budgeting features, you must link all bank accounts and provide extensive personal information including phone number and email. They immediately push credit score checks, car insurance offers, and product recommendations. Very little actual budgeting functionality. Automated categorization is mediocre. Difficult to use for planning future expenses. Only useful if you want credit monitoring and product comparison. Not useful for budgeting. Not recommended.

3. Oportun (spelled Opportun but pronounced Opportune) claims to be a budgeting app but is actually a savings and investing app with an attached bank. The app automatically decides how much money to transfer from your linked accounts into their proprietary bank platform. You cannot control transfer amounts or schedules. The app then suggests investments and moves your money from savings into those investments. This creates obvious conflicts of interest. You have no override capability. For sixty dollars per year, you should have complete control over your money. This app takes control away from you. Not recommended for budgeting purposes.

4. Honey Due is designed specifically for couples to share budgets. If you are not budgeting with a partner, this app is not for you. Even for couples, the partner-heavy focus detracts from core budgeting functionality. Free but ad-supported.

Some features you would want most are buried under extra menus. Clunky user experience. Better partner budgeting options exist in other apps that also work well for individual budgeting.

5. Dollar Bird Pro is marketed as a budgeting app but tracks spending by calendar rather than by category. Seems more geared toward business expense tracking and invoice management than personal budgeting. Could not find actual budget-setting capabilities during testing. Might work for some specific use cases but does not function as a general budgeting tool. Skip this one.
6. Budget Spending Tracker tries to pack too much functionality into a cheap app. The result is a cluttered, confusing interface. Features do not work smoothly. Better free alternatives exist that do less but do it better. Not worth the frustration.
7. Wallet App is only about one year old and feels unfinished. Twenty-two dollars per year is overpriced for what it offers. Basic overview of finances without ability to get into details. Some users report credit card link drops and transaction categorization issues. Needs another year of development before it is competitive. Wait for improvements before trying this one.

When evaluating budgeting apps, watch for these red flags: apps that force you to link bank accounts before you can even see the interface, apps that immediately push credit checks or financial product sales, apps that are actually loan or cash advance services disguised as budgeting tools, apps with terrible user reviews citing frequent bugs or poor customer service, apps that are overpriced compared to competitors with similar features. If you see these red flags, skip that app and try something else.

Choosing Your Budgeting Tool

Now that you have seen the options, how do you choose? Follow this decision process.

First, decide your budget for budgeting software. Are you willing to spend nothing, willing to spend thirty to fifty dollars per year, or willing to spend up to one hundred dollars per year for premium features? Your answer eliminates options and narrows your choices.

Second, decide whether you want to link bank accounts for automatic transaction tracking or whether you prefer manual entry. Automatic is more convenient but requires trusting apps with your banking credentials. Manual gives you complete control and security but requires more effort. Your preference eliminates more options.

Third, decide which features matter most to you. Do you need investment tracking? Bill negotiation? Debt payoff planning? Sharing with a partner? Extremely detailed reporting? Different apps excel at different features. Match your priorities to app strengths.

Fourth, try free trials before committing. Most paid apps offer one-week to one-month free trials. Download two or three apps. Spend a weekend with each. See which interface feels most natural to you. See which one you actually enjoy using. The best app is the one you will use consistently.

Fifth, commit for ninety days minimum. Do not app-hop. Do not switch every two weeks because you saw a feature you liked in a different app. Pick one. Learn it deeply. Use it for ninety days. Give it time to work. If after ninety days you genuinely do not like it, switch. But ninety days minimum. Most people quit apps too early before habits form and before they learn the full functionality.

Here is my personal recommendation based on thirty-five years working with people on budgets: Start with a free app or a low-cost app like GoodBudget, Spending Tracker, or

Today's Budget. Use it for three to six months. Learn budgeting fundamentals. Build tracking habits. Get comfortable with the process. Then, if you feel limited by the free app, upgrade to a premium app like Monarch, YNAB, or Copilot. The premium features will be more valuable after you understand budgeting basics. Jumping straight to premium software when you have never budgeted before often leads to overwhelm and abandonment.

The tool does not make you successful. Your discipline makes you successful. A free app used consistently will produce better results than a premium app used sporadically. Pick something. Commit to it. Use it every single day. That is what matters.

Notice what the tools are actually doing. They are not making decisions for you. They are making your decisions visible. Visibility creates accountability. Accountability creates consistency. Consistency is what separates people who talk about wealth from people who build it.

This is why tools matter—but only in their proper place. They exist to reinforce habits, not replace them.

Beyond Budgeting Apps: Other Essential Tools

Budgeting software is important, but it is not the only tool you need. Here are other resources that support your wealth-building journey.

Spreadsheets

If you do not want to use budgeting apps, spreadsheets work perfectly fine. Microsoft Excel or Google Sheets are powerful budgeting tools if you know how to use them. The advantage of spreadsheets is complete control and customization. You build exactly the tracking system you want. The disadvantage is you do everything manually. No automatic bank syncing. No transaction categorization. You enter everything yourself and create your own formulas.

Spreadsheets work best for people who enjoy detailed control and do not mind manual data entry. If this sounds like you, find a budget spreadsheet template online or build your own. Include columns for date, description, category, amount, and running balance. Create separate sheets for each month. Create a summary sheet that shows yearly totals by category. Use formulas to calculate totals automatically. Review weekly. Reconcile monthly with bank statements.

The discipline of manually entering every transaction forces awareness. You cannot mindlessly swipe a card when you know you will have to type that transaction into a spreadsheet later. The friction is a feature, not a bug. Manual tracking makes you think about every dollar. For some people, this leads to better results than automated tracking.

Cash Envelopes

I covered the cash envelope system in Chapter 3, but I want to emphasize it again here. Cash envelopes are a physical tool, not a digital tool. They work when apps fail for people who struggle with digital money.

Buy a box of letter-size envelopes. Label them with your variable spending categories: groceries, gas, eating out, entertainment, personal care, clothing, miscellaneous. Each pay period, withdraw the cash allocated to each category. Put the cash in the labeled envelopes. Spend only from the envelopes for each category. When an envelope is empty, you are done spending in that category for the month.

Cash envelopes eliminate overspending. You cannot overspend money you do not have. The physical limitation of cash forces discipline. Digital transactions feel abstract. Cash feels real. For people who struggle with credit card overspending or who have no awareness of digital money leaving their account, cash envelopes are transformational.

The downside of cash envelopes is they require carrying cash, which some people find inconvenient or unsafe. They do not work for online purchases. They do not automatically track for you. But the psychological benefit often outweighs these inconveniences. If you have tried apps and failed, try cash envelopes for ninety days. Many people who failed with digital budgeting succeed with physical cash.

Spending Tracking Notebooks

Before apps and spreadsheets existed, people tracked spending in small notebooks. This still works. Buy a pocket-sized notebook. Carry it everywhere. Write down every single expense when it happens. Date, description, amount. At the end of the day, you have a complete record.

The benefit is simplicity. No technology required. No learning curve. Just write. The act of writing forces you to consciously acknowledge every purchase. This awareness alone reduces impulse spending. Studies show people who track spending by hand spend less than people who do not track at all.

At the end of each week, transfer your notebook entries to a spreadsheet or budgeting app for categorization and analysis. Or just add up totals by category in your notebook. Keep notebooks from previous months. Review them quarterly to see patterns.

Spending notebooks work for people who resist technology or who want maximum simplicity. They also work well combined with apps. Use the notebook for immediate tracking throughout the day. Use the app for weekly review and analysis. This combination gives you both immediate awareness and long-term trend analysis.

Bill Payment Calendars

Many people miss bill payments not because they lack money but because they forget due dates. A bill payment calendar solves this problem. Get a large wall calendar or use a digital calendar on your phone. Mark every bill due date. Include the payee name and amount due.

Each pay period, look at your calendar. See which bills are due before your next paycheck. Pay those bills immediately. Mark them as paid on the calendar. This prevents late fees and keeps your credit score healthy. Late fees are wasted money. A thirty-five dollar late fee because you forgot to pay a bill on time is thirty-five dollars you could have saved or used to pay off debt.

Bill payment calendars also help you plan for irregular expenses. If you know your car insurance bill is due in two months, you can save money each month so you have cash ready when the bill arrives. No surprises. No scrambling. Just methodical planning.

Debt Payoff Trackers

If you are eliminating debt, visual progress tracking keeps you motivated. Debt payoff can take years. Without visible progress, you lose motivation. A debt payoff tracker shows you how far you have come.

Create a simple chart. List all your debts with their starting balances. Each month when you make a payment, update the remaining balance. Color in or mark off the portion you paid. Watching the debt shrink visually is psychologically powerful. Celebrate milestones. The first thousand paid off. Halfway done. Seventy-five percent done. Each milestone deserves recognition.

Some people prefer debt thermometers where they color in the thermometer as debt goes down. Some prefer bar graphs. Some prefer just crossing out debt amounts as they are eliminated. Find a visual method that works for you. Put it somewhere visible. Let it motivate you during the long process of debt elimination.

Financial Education Resources

Tools for tracking money are important. Tools for learning about money are equally important. I recommend books, podcasts, and websites that teach financial literacy, investing basics, and wealth-building strategies.

Books I recommend: "The Total Money Makeover" by Dave Ramsey for debt elimination fundamentals. "The Millionaire Next Door" by Thomas Stanley for understanding how real millionaires live and build wealth. "The Richest Man in Babylon" by George Clason for timeless financial wisdom. "I Will Teach You to Be Rich" by Ramit Sethi for practical money management for younger people. "Your Money or Your Life" by Vicki Robin for understanding the relationship between money and life energy.

Read one personal finance book per quarter. Four books per year. In five years, you will have read twenty books on money management. Your financial knowledge will exceed ninety-five percent of the population. Knowledge compounds. Educated decisions compound. Reading compounds your wealth.

Podcasts provide free ongoing education. Find podcasts about budgeting, investing, real estate, entrepreneurship, and wealth building. Listen during your commute or while doing household tasks. Thirty minutes per day is three and a half hours per week. Over one hundred fifty hours per year of financial education for free. This education is worth thousands of dollars but costs nothing except time.

Websites with solid financial information: Investopedia for learning investing terminology. BiggerPockets for real estate investing education. Mr. Money Mustache for extreme frugality and early retirement strategies. The Simple Dollar for practical budgeting advice. Read articles. Join forums. Ask questions. Learn from people who have already achieved what you want to achieve.

Financial education is a tool. Treat it as essential. Invest time in learning. The return on investment is massive. People who understand compound interest, tax advantages, and investment vehicles build wealth faster than people who do not. Knowledge is power. Get knowledge.

Insurance Policies as Financial Tools

Insurance is a defensive tool that protects your wealth from catastrophic loss. You need health insurance, car insurance, homeowners or renters insurance, and life insurance if you have dependents. These insurances are expensive. They are also non-negotiable.

One uninsured medical emergency can bankrupt you. One at-fault car accident without insurance can destroy decades of savings. One house fire without insurance can eliminate your net worth overnight. Insurance prevents these scenarios. Insurance is what allows you to recover from disasters instead of being destroyed by them.

Review your insurance coverage annually. Are your deductibles appropriate? Are you overinsured in some areas and underinsured in others? Shop for better rates every year. Insurance companies raise rates over time betting you will not notice. Shopping annually prevents this. You can often save two hundred to five hundred dollars per year just by getting new quotes and switching companies.

Insurance is a tool for wealth preservation. You build wealth through budgeting and investing. You protect wealth through insurance. Both are necessary. Do not skip insurance to save money. That is gambling with your financial future.

Buy appropriate coverage. Shop for the best rates. Protect what you build.

The Wealth Connection: From Budgeting to Millionaire

Now that you have the tools, let me explain why they matter. Let me show you how budgeting discipline connects directly to building lasting wealth. Most people think budgeting and wealth building are separate topics. They are wrong. Budgeting is wealth building. The discipline you develop through budgeting is exactly the discipline required to become a millionaire.

I have worked as a lender and mortgage banker for thirty-five years. I have met thousands of wealthy people and thousands of broke people. I have reviewed their finances. I have seen their habits. I have watched who succeeds and who fails. The wealthy people all share certain characteristics. The broke people all share different characteristics. Let me tell you what I observed.

Wealthy people track their money obsessively. Every wealthy person I have worked with knows exactly where their money is, how much they have, and where it is going. They do not guess. They do not estimate. They know. They track. They review. They measure. This is the same skill you develop through budgeting. Tracking every dollar in your budget trains you to track every dollar of your investments, every dollar of your business revenue, every dollar everywhere. This awareness is wealth.

Wealthy people live below their means. The millionaires I worked with do not drive luxury cars. They do not live in the biggest houses. They do not wear expensive clothes. They live modestly. They save the difference between their income and their expenses. They invest that difference. The discipline of living below your means that you develop through budgeting is exactly the discipline that allows wealth accumulation. You cannot become wealthy if you spend everything you earn. Budgeting teaches you to spend less than you earn. This is wealth building.

Wealthy people delay gratification. They want things just like everyone else. They choose not to buy those things because they prefer future wealth over present consumption. The discipline of saying no to impulse purchases in your budget trains you to say no to lifestyle inflation as your income grows. Most people increase spending when income increases. Wealthy people do not. They save and invest increases. Budgeting trains delayed gratification. Delayed gratification creates wealth.

Wealthy people avoid debt. The wealthy people I worked with either had no debt or used debt strategically for appreciating assets only. They did not finance cars. They did not carry credit card balances. They did not buy things they could not afford. The discipline of eliminating consumer debt through your budget teaches you to avoid debt permanently. Avoiding debt means keeping all your income instead of sending portions to creditors. This is wealth.

Wealthy people automate their savings and investments. They pay themselves first. Money gets moved to savings and investments before they can spend it. This is the exact system Chapter 3 taught you through the allocation method. Pay yourself first. Automate transfers. Build wealth systematically. Wealthy people have done this for decades. You are now doing the same thing. This automation is wealth building on autopilot.

Wealthy people plan long-term. They think in decades, not days. They make decisions today based on where they want to be in ten years. Your personal business plan from Chapter 1 with three, five, seven, and ten-year projections trains you to think like wealthy people think. You are no longer reacting to today's emotions. You are executing a long-term plan. This is how wealth gets built.

Wealthy people invest consistently. They put money into assets that they appreciate. Stocks, real estate, businesses. They do this month after month, year after year, decade after decade. The money you save through your budget is the money you invest. Budgeting creates the surplus that investing requires. Without budgeting discipline, there is no surplus. Without surplus, there is no investing. Without investing, there is no wealth. Budgeting is the foundation of all investing.

Here is the wealth-building formula: Earn income. Spend less than you earn through disciplined budgeting. Save the difference. Invest the savings in appreciating assets. Repeat for decades. Let compound interest work. This is how ordinary people become millionaires. This is how you become wealthy.

The budgeting discipline you developed through this book is not about restriction. It is about wealth. Every dollar you did not waste on low-priority expenses is a dollar you invested in your future. Every time you said no to impulse purchases, you said yes to financial freedom. Every month you tracked your spending, you built the habits that millionaires have. You are not just budgeting. You are training yourself to think and act like wealthy people think and act.

Let me give you numbers to show how budgeting discipline creates wealth. You are thirty years old. You make forty thousand dollars per year. Through disciplined budgeting, you reduce expenses by three hundred dollars per month. You invest that three hundred dollars per month in a retirement account earning an average of eight percent annually. You do this consistently for thirty-five years until you are sixty-five.

At age sixty-five, you have six hundred fifty thousand dollars. You created over half a million dollars of wealth by budgeting three hundred dollars per month. Three hundred dollars per month seems small. Over decades, it becomes transformational. This is compound interest. This is wealth building. This is what budgeting discipline creates.

Now imagine you save five hundred dollars per month through even more disciplined budgeting. Same scenario. I am thirty years old. Eight percent annual return. Thirty-five years of consistency. At age sixty-five, you have one million eighty thousand dollars. You are a millionaire. You created a seven-figure net worth by budgeting five hundred dollars per month. This is not a theory. This is math. This is what happens when budgeting discipline meets compound interest over time.

Most people never become wealthy because they never budget. They earn good incomes. They spend everything. They have nothing left to invest. They work for forty years and retire with almost nothing. They wonder why they are broke while their income is good. The answer is simple: they lacked budgeting discipline. They spent instead of saved. They consumed instead of invested. They lived for today instead of planning for tomorrow.

You will not make that mistake. You have the discipline now. You have the tools now. You have the plan now. You will budget consistently. You will save the surplus. You will invest for decades. You will build wealth. You will retire comfortably. You will leave an inheritance for your children. You will achieve financial freedom. This is what budgeting discipline creates.

The connection between budgeting and wealth is direct. Budgeting is not separate from wealth building. Budgeting is the first step of wealth building. Budgeting is the foundation everything else stands on. Without budgeting, there is no surplus. Without surplus, there is no investing. Without investing, there is no compound growth. Without compound growth, there is no wealth. Budgeting is where wealth begins.

Let me give you numbers to show how budgeting discipline creates wealth. You are thirty years old. You make forty thousand dollars per year. Through disciplined budgeting, you reduce expenses by three hundred dollars per month. You invest that three hundred dollars per month in a retirement account earning an average of eight percent annually. You do this consistently for thirty-five years until you are sixty-five.

At age sixty-five, you have six hundred fifty thousand dollars. You created over half a million dollars of wealth by budgeting three hundred dollars per month. Three hundred dollars per month seems small. Over decades, it becomes transformational. This is compound interest. This is wealth building. This is what budgeting discipline creates.

Now imagine you save five hundred dollars per month through even more disciplined budgeting. Same scenario. Thirty years old. Eight percent annual return. Thirty-five years of consistency. At age sixty-five, you have one million eighty thousand dollars. You are a millionaire. You created a seven-figure net worth by budgeting five hundred dollars per month. This is not a theory. This is math. This is what happens when budgeting discipline meets compound interest over time.

Most people never become wealthy because they never budget. They earn good incomes. They spend everything. They have nothing left to invest. They work for forty years and retire with almost nothing. They wonder why they are broke while their income was good. The answer is simple: they lacked budgeting discipline. They spent instead of saved. They consumed instead of invested. They lived for today instead of planning for tomorrow.

You will not make that mistake. You have the discipline now. You have the tools now. You have the plan now. You will budget consistently. You will save the surplus. You will invest for decades. You will build wealth. You will retire comfortably. You will leave an inheritance for your children. You will achieve financial freedom. This is what budgeting discipline creates.

Wealth is not a single event. It is a sequence.

It begins with awareness—knowing where your money is going. Awareness leads to control. Control leads to margin. Margin creates investable cash. Investable cash leads to ownership. Ownership leads to stability. Stability opens the door to opportunity. Opportunity, when stewarded well, becomes legacy.

This is the wealth connection.

Budgeting is not the destination. It is the discipline that makes the destination possible. Homeownership, investing, and long-term security are not accidents. They are the cumulative result of thousands of small, aligned decisions made visible and reinforced by systems.

Tools help you stay aligned. They turn intention into routine. Routine into progress. Progress into wealth.

Staying Accountable Over the Long Term

You have tools. You understand the wealth connection. Now you need systems to stay accountable for years, not just months. Budgeting for ninety days is good. Budgeting for ninety years is wealth. How do you maintain discipline over decades?

First, automate everything you can. Automate your savings transfers. Automate your investment contributions. Automate your bill payments. Automation removes the need for willpower. Automation removes the opportunity for failure. The money moves before you can make a bad decision. Set up automation once. Let it run forever. This is how you budget for decades without constant active management.

Second, review your budget regularly but not obsessively. Weekly reviews keep you on track. Monthly reconciliations catch problems early. Quarterly assessments allow big-picture analysis. Annual reviews incorporate major life changes. Do not check your budget multiple times per day. That creates stress and burnout. Once per week is sufficient for daily spending monitoring. Once per month is sufficient for detailed analysis. Find a rhythm that keeps you informed without consuming your life.

Third, celebrate milestones. When you eliminate a debt, celebrate. When you hit a savings goal, celebrate. When you reach net worth milestones, celebrate. Celebration reinforces positive behavior. Celebration keeps you motivated through the long journey. Most people only focus on how far they have to go. Also focus on how far you have come. Both matter. Acknowledge progress. Reward yourself appropriately. Keep moving forward.

Fourth, revisit your mission, vision, and goals annually. Your financial why from Chapter 1 is not static. Life changes. Priorities shift. Goals evolve. Review your mission statement every year. Does it still resonate? Does it still drive you? If not, update it. Review your vision statement. Is that still the future you want? If not, adjust it. Review your goals. Did you achieve some? Great. Set new ones. Did some become irrelevant? Fine. Replace them. Your personal business plan is a living document. Keep it current. Keep it motivating.

Fifth, stay connected to your accountability partner. Weekly check-ins might drop to monthly after the first year. That is fine. Monthly might drop to quarterly after several years. That is fine too. But never drop accountability completely. Always have someone who knows your goals and checks your progress. Accountability prevents backsliding. Accountability keeps you honest. Maintain the relationship. Maintain the check-ins. Maintain accountability.

Sixth, continue financial education throughout your life. You read books in the early years to learn budgeting basics. Continue reading books about advanced topics. Investing strategies. Tax optimization. Real estate. Business. Estate planning. Wealth preservation. Financial education never ends. Markets change. Laws change. Strategies evolve. Stay educated. Stay current. Stay sharp. Knowledge today prevents expensive mistakes tomorrow.

Seventh, adjust for major life changes immediately. You get married. Combine finances. Update your budget. You have a baby. Add childcare costs. Update your budget. You buy a house. Add mortgage and maintenance. Update your budget. You get divorced. Split finances. Update your budget. You get a raise. Increase your savings percentage. Update your budget. You lose a job. Cut discretionary spending immediately. Update your budget. Life changes require budget changes. React quickly. Adjust completely. Do not let your budget become outdated and irrelevant. Keep it aligned with current reality.

Eighth, teach others what you learned. When you achieve financial success through budgeting, share your knowledge. Teach your children. Help your friends. Mentor someone who is where you used to be. Teaching reinforces your own knowledge. Teaching creates accountability. Teaching gives your success meaning beyond personal gain. The principles in this book changed your life. Pass them forward. Help others change their lives too.

Budgeting discipline maintained over decades creates generational wealth. You will not just change your own life. You will change your children's lives. You will model financial discipline for them. You will teach them to budget. You will leave them an inheritance. Your grandchildren will benefit from decisions you make today. This is legacy. This is an impact. This is what budgeting discipline creates over the long term.

Your Final Assignment

You finished the book. You learned the system. You have the tools. Now you must commit to lifetime implementation. Here is your final assignment.

First, choose your primary budgeting tool today. Download an app or set up a spreadsheet. Spend one hour learning the interface. Enter your first budget. Begin tracking immediately. Do not wait. Do not research more options endlessly. Pick one. Start today.

Second, implement every component of your personal business plan from Chapter 1. Review your mission, vision, goals, projections, core values, and belief statement. Make sure they are written down and visible. Commit them to memory. Let them guide every financial decision going forward.

Third, complete your one-month spending audit from Chapter 2 if you have not already. You cannot build an accurate budget without understanding current spending. Track for thirty full days. Categorize everything. Build your budget on facts.

Fourth, implement the allocation system from Chapter 3. Allocate your income to high priority, medium priority, and low priority expenses plus savings and debt elimination. Use cash envelopes for variable spending categories. Automate savings and bill payments. Get your budget operational.

Fifth, execute the income strategies from Chapter 4 that fit your situation. Start a one side income stream this month. Commit to it for six months. Invest the extra income into savings or debt elimination. Do not let lifestyle inflation consume income increases.

Sixth, implement the expense cuts from Chapter 5. Choose three major cuts to make this week. Cancel subscriptions. Downgrade services. Stop eating out. Save the difference.

Redirect savings to emergency fund or debt elimination. Cut aggressively for the first six months. Get momentum.

Seventh, review the seventeen mistakes from Chapter 6 monthly for the first year. Check yourself against the list. Are you making any of these mistakes? If yes, fix them immediately. Do not repeat mistakes month after month. Learn and improve continuously.

Eighth, schedule your weekly and monthly budget reviews. Sunday evening for weekly review. Last day of the month for monthly reconciliation. Put these appointments in your calendar. Treat them as non-negotiable. Consistent review is what makes budgeting work long-term.

Ninth, schedule quarterly meetings with your accountability partner. First quarter review in three months. Discuss progress. Identify challenges. Celebrate wins. Adjust goals if needed. Maintain accountability throughout the journey.

Tenth, commit to one year of perfect budget execution. One year of tracking every dollar. One year of staying within spending limits. One year of hitting savings goals. One year of avoiding new debt. One year of building the habits that create wealth. After one year of consistency, budgeting becomes automatic. The discipline becomes permanent. The results become undeniable. Give yourself one year of total commitment. One year changes everything.

You have everything you need now. You have the foundation. You have the tracking system. You have the allocation method. You have income strategies. You have expense cutting techniques. You have mistake avoidance training. You have tools. You have the wealth connection understanding. You have accountability structures.

The only missing ingredient is your commitment. Will you do this? Will you track every dollar? Will you stick to your budget? Will you make sacrifices now for wealth later? Will you live like no one else now so you can live like no one else later?

Most people will read this book and change nothing. They will agree with the principles. They will like the ideas. They will do nothing. They will stay broke. They will wonder why their finances never improve. They will blame circumstances. They will blame the economy. They will blame everyone except themselves.

You are not most people. You will do the work. You will implement the system. You will build the discipline. You will create wealth. You will achieve financial freedom. You will retire comfortably. You will leave a legacy.

This is not motivation. This is commitment. Commit now. Start today. Change your life.

CONCLUSION: The Power of the Budget

You reached the end. You have the complete system. Seven chapters. Thousands of words. Decades of experience distilled into practical steps. Everything you need to transform your financial life is in this book.

Let me remind you why this matters.

A budget is not about restrictions. A budget is about power. The power to control your money instead of letting your money control you. The power to make decisions based on your goals instead of based on your emotions. The power to say no to things that do not matter and yes to things that do. The power to build wealth instead of wondering where your money went. This is power. This is freedom. This is why we budget.

Only forty percent of American households have a budget. Sixty percent spend without a plan. Those sixty percent live paycheck to paycheck. They carry debt. They have no savings. They stress about money constantly. They will work until they die because they never built wealth. They lack power over their financial lives.

You are now forty percent. You have a plan. You have a

budget. You have a system. You have power. You joined the minority who control their money and build wealth. This minority retires early. This minority lives without financial stress. This minority leaves inheritances. This minority has options. You are now part of this group.

But knowledge without action means nothing. You can read this book ten times and memorize every chapter. If you do not implement, you will stay broke. Reading changes nothing. Action changes everything. You must do the work. You must track your spending. You must follow your budget. You must make sacrifices. You must stay disciplined. You must maintain consistency for years.

This is hard. Nobody said wealth building was easy. Nobody said budgeting was fun. Nobody said discipline was comfortable. Hard is okay. Hard means most people will not do it. Hard means less competition. Hard means bigger rewards for those who persist. You will persist. You will do what is hard now. You will enjoy what is easy later.

I have spent thirty-five years helping people buy homes and build wealth. I have seen who succeeds and who fails. The ones who succeed are not smarter. They are not luckier. They do not earn more. They simply have more discipline. They follow a plan. They budget consistently. They make tough choices. They delay gratification. They persist through difficulty. They win because they do what losing people will not do.

You have everything you need now. You have the foundation. You have the tracking system. You have the Income Blueprint. You have the Allocation System. You have the Elimination List for cutting expenses. You have mistake-avoidance training. You have tools. You have the wealth connection. You have accountability structures. The only missing ingredient is your commitment.

Start today. Not Monday. Not next month. Not when life gets less busy. Today. Open a budgeting app right now. Track your first expense. Write your mission statement. Do something. Take one action. Begin the journey. Momentum starts with one step. Take the step.

Commit to ninety days of perfect execution. Three months of tracking every dollar, following your budget, hitting your savings goals, and avoiding new debt. After ninety days, you will have built habits. Habits become automatic. Automatic becomes effortless. Effortlessness becomes permanent. Give yourself ninety days. Change your life.

I believe you can do this. I have seen thousands of people transform their finances through budgeting discipline. People who made less money than you. People who started with more debt than you. People who had more obstacles than you. They succeeded. You can too. You will too.

If you take nothing else from this chapter, remember this: tools are not about convenience—they are about continuity. They help you stay the course long after motivation fades.

When you combine a clear foundation, honest tracking, a strong income strategy, disciplined allocation, intentional pruning, and awareness of common mistakes, tools become the final support structure that holds everything together.

This is how the Power Budget moves from a monthly exercise to a lifelong system. This is how discipline becomes ownership. This is how order becomes opportunity. And this is how financial stewardship becomes something far greater than numbers—it becomes a legacy.

Go build wealth. Go achieve financial freedom. Go create the life you want. The power is yours now. Use it.

DID YOU ENJOY THIS BOOK?

I sure hope so!

Please join our family and write a review. Reviews are the "tip jar" of the book publishing industry. New readers weigh reviews heavily in deciding to make a purchase. You being so generous as to share your experience is the lifeblood of the success of "Run Your Household Like A Business" To do this please scan the QR code below

I appreciate you!
Eric Lawrence Frazier

BECOME A MEMBER TODAY

Why Become a Member of The Power Is Now Media?

Unlock exclusive access to the most powerful real estate, mortgage, credit, and wealth-building content in the industry.

For a limited time, become a member for only $10/month or $60/year. Your membership delivers undeniable value, insider access, and proven tools to help you buy, sell, invest, and build wealth with confidence.

Membership Benefits

Exclusive Streaming & Shows

- Unlimited access to The Power Is Now TV Network library of hundreds of shows, podcasts, and webinars.
- Daily programming on homeownership, real estate investing, mortgages, credit, and financial literacy (Federal Reserve, 2024)[1].

- Member-only live streams and roundtable discussions with top industry leaders.

Free Digital Resources

- Real estate eBooks, guides, and reports on buying, selling, investing, and credit strategies (Consumer Financial Protection Bureau, 2023)[7].
- Buyer & Seller Guides, HUD Homes Guide, and Foreclosure Market Reports, updated quarterly (U.S. Department of Housing and Urban Development, 2025)[55].
- Access to The Power Is Now Media Resource Library of downloadable content.

Magazines & Newsletters

- Complimentary subscription to The Power Is Now National Real Estate Magazine.
- Complimentary subscription to The Power Is Now HUD Homes for Sale Magazine.
- Complimentary subscription to The Power Is Now TV Guide Magazine.
- Complimentary subscription to Faith, Family & Finance Magazine.
- Weekly newsletters with videos, infographics, and market insights (Federal Reserve Bank of New York, 2023)[9].

Member Engagement

- Invitations to attend and participate in live recordings of the Real Estate Roundtable and Business Roundtable.

- Networking opportunities with agents, lenders, investors, and entrepreneurs nationwide.
- Priority access to quarterly webinars for first-time homebuyers, investors, and asset managers (U.S. Department of Housing and Urban Development, 2025)[55].
- Monthly group coaching sessions on Personal Finance, Real Estate, Mortgage, and Media (Federal Reserve, 2024)[1].

Discounts & Savings

- Member-only discounts on media services (podcast hosting, YouTube TV production, private-label magazines, website redesigns, social media management).
- Exclusive pricing on advertising, sponsorships, and coaching programs.

Community & Recognition

- Become part of a national network of professionals and consumers committed to real estate wealth-building.
- Opportunities to feature your story, listings, or business on The Power Is Now TV Network.

Special Membership Offer

Join now at www.thepowerisnow.com

Special Launch Price: $10/month or $60/year (limited-time offer through year-end).

BECOME A MEMBER TODAY

Regular Price: $50/month or $325/year.

Don't wait—membership pays for itself many times over.

For over 16 years, The Power Is Now has been dedicated to educating and empowering people in real estate, mortgage, credit, and wealth-building (Consumer Financial Protection Bureau, 2023)[7]. Now, through our membership program, you can unlock exclusive access to everything we offer.

For only $10 a month or $60 a year, you'll get unlimited access to hundreds of shows on The Power Is Now TV Network, free eBooks and real estate guides, four magazine subscriptions, weekly newsletters, and live roundtable access with industry leaders. You'll also enjoy discounts on media services, group coaching, and the chance to network with professionals across the country.

But here's the best part—you'll be part of a movement. A national community committed to real estate wealth-building, financial literacy, and creating generational wealth (Federal Reserve, 2024)[1].

So go to www.thepowerisnow.com today and become a member. This special pricing is only available until the end of the year. Join us, and let's build wealth together.

ABOUT THE AUTHOR

Mr. Eric Lawrence Frazier, MBA, is the President and CEO of The Power Is Now Media, a national multimedia company dedicated to real estate education, empowerment, and thought leadership. Through its expansive platform —comprising the Power Is Now website (www.thepowerisnow.com), national podcast networks, social media channels, and live-stream television platforms—the company delivers timely, authoritative content on real estate, lending, economics, and government policy.

In addition to leading the media network, Mr. Frazier serves as the Publisher and Editor-in-Chief of The Power Is Now Publishing, which produces books and magazines dedicated to real estate, financial literacy, and wealth building. Since its founding, the publishing division has created a wide range of educational materials, including The Power Is Now Magazines, a suite of online real estate publications launched in 2013 that feature market insights, national news, and educational resources for both homebuyers and professionals.

Mr. Frazier is a graduate of the University of Redlands in Redlands, California, where he earned a Master of Business Administration (MBA) with an emphasis in Finance as well as a Bachelor of Science in Business Administration and Management. He has lectured on the U.S. mortgage crisis at the University of California, Riverside, addressing international business leaders from India, and has served as an adjunct professor.

With nearly four decades of expertise in mortgage banking, Mr. Frazier is nationally recognized for his leadership in origination, underwriting, operations, management, and marketing. He has also built a distinguished career in real estate sales and brokerage, holding a California real estate license for over thirty years and a broker's license (#01143484) for more than twenty-eight years. Together with his wife, he founded Frazier Group Realty (www.fraziergrouprealty.com), a full-service, family-owned real estate company based in Riverside, California.

Mr. Frazier's professional leadership extends into numerous industry associations. He is the former President of the Orange County Realtist chapter of the National Association of Real Estate Brokers (NAREB) and a former Director of the California Association of Real Estate Brokers. He has also served as Vice President of the Orange County chapter of the National Association of Hispanic Real Estate Professionals (NAHREP) and as an Advisory Board Member of the Orange County chapter of the Asian Real Estate Association of America (AREAA). He has served on the Board of Directors of the Riverside Fair Housing Council, was a past member of the Pacific West Association of Realtors, and is currently a member of the Inland Valley Association of Realtors (IVAR).

Beyond real estate, Mr. Frazier is deeply engaged in civic and community leadership. He has served on the Board of Directors of Project Tomorrow (www.tomorrow.org), a national nonprofit organization dedicated to education. He is an active member of the 100 Black Men of America, the NAACP, and the National Association of Mortgage Brokers. He is also the past President and Director of the State of California African American Museum (www.caamuseum.org).

His spiritual leadership is rooted in the church. Mr. Frazier is a pastor and leads The Power Is Now Ministries, a ministry of the North Fontana Church, a 501(c)(non-profit) organization, where he continues to serve through teaching, outreach, and mentorship.

A man of diverse talents, Mr. Frazier is also an author, blogger, poet, singer, songwriter, motivational speaker, business consultant, and coach to both for-profit and nonprofit organizations, as well as a personal financial coach. He is the published author of six books spanning poetry, African American wealth, credit, and business. His personal interests include golf, running, and jazz music.

Mr. Frazier is especially committed to mentorship, striving to be a role model for African American men and dedicating time to coaching young people and adults. His greatest joy, however, is found in family. He has been married to the love of his life, Ruby, for over forty years, and together they have raised four accomplished daughters. His three eldest daughters hold master's degrees in management and business, while his youngest has earned a bachelor's degree in apparel merchandising and management.

All of Mr. Frazier's professional accomplishments, affiliations, and ongoing work can be found at **www.linkedin.com/in/ericfrazier**.

FOLLOW ME ON SOCIAL MEDIA

LET'S CONNECT ON LINKEDIN

ABOUT THE POWER IS NOW MEDIA

The Power Is Now Media is an online multimedia company founded in 2009 by Eric L. Frazier MBA, headquartered in Riverside, California. We are advocates for homeownership, wealth building, and financial literacy. We create and publish original educational content about real estate through nationally syndicated Radio, Podcasts, Magazines, TV, Social Media, Streaming platforms, and special online seminars and webinars. We are an online platform and resource for everyone to learn about homeownership, housing, loan programs, and down payment assistance to achieve financial literacy and the American dream of homeownership. We are supported by housing finance agencies, real estate associations, and civic, religious, and community organizations. We help them amplify their voice about the services and programs they offer in lending, housing, and homeownership. Visit us at www.thepowerisnow.com

The Mission of the Power is Now Media is to inspire and educate consumers and real estate professionals to build wealth through the acquisition, management, and sale of real estate with information and support we provide via our website, live and on-demand TV, and social media platforms that empower everyone to own real estate now and achieve the American dream of homeownership. Our company slogan is "We are leading the conversation about real homeownership."

The Power Is Now Media corporate office is located at 3739 6th Street, Riverside, CA 92501. Telephone/Fax: 800-401-8994. Eric Lawrence Frazier MBA is a California Licensed Loan Originator (NMLS License #461807) and Real Estate Broker (License #O1148434).

www.ingramcontent.com/pod-product-compliance
Lightning Source LLC
Chambersburg PA
CBHW071305110426
42743CB00042B/1174